The Colonial Williamsburg Tavern Cookbook

The Colonial Williamsburg Tavern Cookbook

The Colonial Williamsburg Foundation

Recipes Developed by JOHN R. GONZALES
Edited by CHARLES PIERCE
Photographs by TOM ECKERLE
Photographs Produced by JOHN MARTIN TAYLOR

CLARKSON POTTER/PUBLISHERS
New York

in association with

The Colonial Williamsburg Foundation
Williamsburg, Virginia

Published by Clarkson Potter/Publishers in association with The Colonial
Williamsburg Foundation. Clarkson Potter/Publishers, New York, New York.
Member of the Crown Publishing Group.

Random House, Inc. New York, Toronto, London, Sydney, Auckland
www.randomhouse.com

CLARKSON N. POTTER is a trademark and POTTER and colophon are
registered trademarks of Random House, Inc.

Printed in China

Design by Maggie Hinders

Library of Congress Cataloging-in-Publication Data
The Colonial Williamsburg tavern cookbook / the Colonial Williamsburg
Foundation—1st ed.
p.   cm.
1. Cookery, American.   2. Cookery–Virginia–Williamsburg.   3. Taverns
(Inns)–Virginia–Williamsburg.   I. Colonial Williamsburg Foundation.
TX715.T218 2000
641.5973–dc21   00-035632

ISBN 0-609-60286-1

10   9   8   7   6   5   4   3   2   1

First Edition

Contents

Introduction

B EFORE leaving Williamsburg on April 8, 1772, George Washington stopped by Christiana Campbell's Tavern and paid Mrs. Campbell for expenses charged against his account while he was in town that spring. With a quill pen, Washington wrote out a receipt for the seven pounds, seven shillings, and sixpence he owed, and she signed it "C Campbell." This scrap of paper is one of Colonial Williamsburg's most treasured documents.

Washington joined fellow members of the House of Burgesses and friends to dine, play cards, or discuss the affairs of the day over a glass of claret at Mrs. Campbell's twenty-two times between March 2 and April 9 that spring. He "Dined at Mrs. Campbells and went to the Play—then to Mrs. Campbells again" twice during the week of April 3. Curiously, he did not visit Jane Vobe's new tavern at the "Sign of the King's Arms" in 1772.

Locals went to taverns year-round. Like English inns, public houses in Williamsburg customarily were a male domain. The number of customers increased during Publick Times, the month or so each spring and fall when the General Court convened and the General Assembly was sometimes in session. Planters, politicians, lawyers, merchants, ship captains, artisans, actors, clergymen, college professors, government clerks and officials, and an occasional foreign traveler could all be found in the public rooms of Williamsburg taverns.

Women who sold produce at the market occasionally stopped at Chowning's Tavern near Market Square to quench their thirst with a pint of small beer or have something to eat before returning home. Few women traveled far enough to need lodging at a tavern, however. When husbands came to Williamsburg on business, wives ordinarily stayed home to tend the children, manage the store or trade shop, or oversee plantation operations.

Although women rarely frequented taverns, men and women of both races worked in them. A successful tavern keeper needed an agreeable personality, good health, and sound business skills. It helped to have a wife who could oversee and often lend a hand with cooking, cleaning, laundry, and marketing. In large public houses like the King's Arms, white male barkeepers dispensed drinks and kept accounts, slave men cared for customers' horses, carted goods, and did most of the heavy work, and teenage slave boys waited on customers and ran errands. Slave women and girls prepared meals, cleaned the rooms, and did the washing. At more modest taverns like the one operated by Josiah Chowning, family members worked alongside one or two slaves.

Colonial laws set maximum prices for everyday meals, alcoholic drinks, lodging, and care for horses, granted local courts authority to license operators, and did not allow patrons to "drink more than is necessary" on the Sabbath. Legislation barred those who could not be sued in court—indentured servants, slaves, and seamen without written permission from their captain—from going to public houses and protected taverners from damages caused by disorderly customers.

College regulations forbade William and Mary students from frequenting taverns unless accompanied by an older friend or family member. Then as now, students sometimes broke the rules. "I send inclosed ... the cash to disburse [my son's] college expenses and to pay £6.13.0 a Balance due to Mrs. Jane Vobe [operator of the King's Arms Tavern] as per inclosed account.... [my son] must be restrained in every matter from hence ... [and] be confined to College and to College Rules," wrote Robert Carter of Nomini Hall plantation to the president of the College of William and Mary in 1779.

What and how much people ate in taverns depended on their social and economic standing. Storekeepers along Duke of Gloucester Street stocked imported capers and olives, dried currants and gooseberries, cheeses from England, and other delicacies. The gentry could afford such treats, but everyday customers—those of the lower and middling sort—expected hearty victuals served up plain rather than an elegant repast. The fixed-price dinners served in the public rooms early in the afternoon included roasted, stewed, or fried meat, poultry, or fish, potatoes and other seasonal vegetables, and bread. Breakfast, about 8 A.M., generally consisted of sliced cold meat or hash, breads, and beverages such as chocolate, tea, and coffee. In cold weather, hominy, a hot cereal made from coarsely ground cornmeal, was also consumed. Supper, a light meal that often consisted of leftovers from dinner, was eaten around 8 P.M. Small beer and cider accompanied ordinary meals.

Keepers of large taverns provided affluent male patrons with special dinners at which they entertained friends and guests. Elaborate symmetrical arrays of food showed the dishes off properly. A Virginia ham was placed at the top of the table; a large joint such as saddle of mutton or leg of lamb at the bottom. Platters of roast fowl went in the center. Vegetables and casseroles appeared along the sides and in the corners; small dishes containing sauces, pickles, and condiments were arranged decoratively. Guests drank imported wines and ales. By 1770, the second, or dessert, course featured sweetmeats, jellies, syllabubs, cakes, pies or tarts, and puddings. Fruits and nuts concluded these lavish meals that sometimes lasted for several hours.

Taverns at
Colonial Williamsburg
Today

COLONIAL WILLIAMSBURG'S operating taverns—Christiana Campbell's, Chowning's, the King's Arms, and Shields—re-create the tastes, smells, and sounds that eighteenth-century visitors to Williamsburg and townspeople experienced. Visitors sample foods suggestive of the past but that suit modern appetites. Guests dine amid authentically reproduced furnishings and accessories, including tablewares, much like those used by their eighteenth-century counterparts. Careful attention to every detail is also reflected in the exteriors of the four re-created taverns.

Each tavern bears the name of the keeper who operated it in the eighteenth century. With the exception of Chowning's, each has been reconstructed on its original foundations. Deeds and other court records, insurance policies, estate inventories, comments in diaries and letters, financial accounts, newspaper advertisements, architectural details from surviving buildings, and archaeological evidence shed light on the lives of the individuals who kept these taverns and the customers who frequented them.

CHOWNING'S TAVERN

Chowning's Tavern, which reopened to the public in 1941 and is little changed today, was Colonial Williamsburg's first operating tavern. Although it was reconstructed on eighteenth-century foundations, researchers have since discovered that a store and dwelling occupied this site at the time Josiah Chowning ran a tavern nearby. The interior details were patterned after alehouses in England. Sturdy tables, chairs, and benches create an air of rustic simplicity where common folk would have been welcome. The delft china that features a blue-and-yellow peacock is based on shards of dinnerware excavated at the site of a similar tavern.

Folks like Josiah Chowning who lacked the capital to buy a building in which to keep a tavern often found that running a hostelry in rented property could be a precarious business. About eighteen months after Chowning announced the opening of his tavern in the *Virginia Gazette* in October 1766, another aspiring keeper advertised that he had "opened TAVERN in the house formerly occupied by Mr. *Chowning*." No one knows why Josiah gave up tavern keeping.

KING'S ARMS TAVERN

Opened as an operating tavern in 1951, the King's Arms represents the upper echelon of Williamsburg's early hostelries. Its architectural features and furnishings replicate the elegant parlors and dining rooms of Virginia's planter class. Widow Jane Vobe sought to attract the elite to her new establishment, announcing in the *Gazette* that she had "just opened Tavern opposite to the Raleigh, at the Sign of The King's Arms" in February 1772. In addition to George Washington, Mrs. Vobe numbered Revolutionary War Generals Thomas Nelson and Baron von Steuben among her patrons.

The early archaeological investigations of this site, which were concerned primarily with locating building foundations, did not capture shards that would have indicated the type of china Mrs. Vobe used. The transfer-printed pattern with the royal arms reproduced on the dinnerware used at the King's Arms today is a composite design similar to fashionable creamware excavated at other 1770s sites in Williamsburg.

Recent redecoration drew on the latest curatorial research to make each space in the tavern represent how Mrs. Vobe's customers used that room for dining, drinking, gambling, or sleeping. Some guests dine in rooms in the adjacent reconstructed Purdie House, home of *Virginia Gazette* printer Alexander Purdie, his wife, Peachy, and the three Purdie boys.

Jane Vobe's tavern-keeping experience began around 1750 when she helped her husband, Thomas Vobe, operate a small hostelry. Thomas died soon afterward. Although some widows of tavern keepers remarried, Mrs. Vobe took advantage of the right to make decisions herself that her widowed status conferred and continued the business.

The widow Vobe quickly attracted a loyal following; by the mid-1760s, her establishment was described as being "where all the best people resorted." When a former storehouse opposite the Raleigh Tavern became available, she renovated and enlarged the building and converted it into a tavern that she named the King's Arms. That name lost favor when hostilities with Great Britain broke out, and by 1776 her establishment began

to be called "Mrs. Vobe's Tavern." Jane Vobe remained in Williamsburg after the capital moved to Richmond in 1780, then relocated across the river from the new capital in 1786.

CHRISTIANA CAMPBELL'S TAVERN

Colonial Williamsburg named its third operating tavern, which opened in 1956, for Christiana Campbell, Jane Vobe's competitor for nearly thirty years. Archaeological evidence, a detailed account of repairs to the building, and a nineteenth-century insurance policy provided clues about the original building. References to Mrs. Campbell's customers indicated that merchants, politicians, and the lower gentry frequented her establishment, so modest, less fashionable furnishings were chosen to refurnish her tavern. Delft tablewares with a distinctive squirrel pattern are based on shards dating from the period when Mrs. Campbell was in business.

Christiana, the daughter of Williamsburg tavern keeper John Burdett, married Dr. Ebenezer Campbell and moved to Petersburg, Virginia. Dr. Campbell soon died, so the young widow, baby Ebenezer, and toddler Molly returned to Williamsburg where she took up tavern keeping, her father's occupation. Christiana Campbell rented property, moved her business as better locations became available, and eventually bought the tavern that bore her name on Waller Street east of the Capitol. The widow Campbell chose to retire after Richmond became the capital.

Assuming that Mrs. Campbell was still in business, Yorktown merchant Alexander Macaulay and his wife planned to stay the night at her tavern in February 1783. The couple barged into the parlor without knocking and were confronted by the irate Widow Campbell, who told them sharply, "I dont keep a house of entertainment, nor have not for some years." Macaulay repaid Christiana for her lack of hospitality by noting that "our Landladys looks were not more inviting than her House. Figure to yourself a little old Woman, about four feet high; & equally thick, a little turn up Pug nose, a mouth screw'd up to one side; in short, nothing in any part of her appearance in the least inviting."

SHIELDS TAVERN

Shields, which became an operating tavern in 1989, is one of the best documented reconstructed buildings in the Historic Area. Researchers relied on both archaeological and documentary evidence to re-create the interior of the building. The detailed room-by-room inventory of the furnishings, taken after keeper James Shields died in 1751, enabled the rooms to be decorated as they were in the eighteenth century. The distinctive fish pattern on the delft tablewares at Shields Tavern comes from ceramic fragments excavated behind the tavern.

Jean Marot, the future father-in-law of James Shields, bought the property in 1708. Taking advantage of the convenient location near the Capitol, within two years Marot doubled the tavern's size, increased the stock of liquors and wines, and attracted a clientele that included leading citizens of the town and colony. Marot died suddenly in 1717. Although the tavern remained in operation for thirty-five years, subsequent keepers were not as successful as he had been in attracting elite customers.

James Shields married Anne Marot, renovated the building sometime in the 1740s, and moved his family into the tavern. When James died in 1750, Anne Marot Shields had five children to support. She operated the tavern for only six months before marrying competitor Henry Wetherburn, a recent widower. While love may have been a factor, the marriage was clearly one of convenience: Anne's children got a stepfather, Henry acquired a wife to oversee the domestic work, and the new partners eliminated a rival tavern keeper.

The Colonial Williamsburg Tavern Cookbook

Appetizers
and
First Courses

THE bite-size tidbits that accompany pre-dinner drinks and the light foods that make up the first courses of dinners today were not served in colonial Virginia. Instead, the host and hostess sipped punch or wine with their guests in the parlor of a gentry home while the wait staff placed the first course on the dining table. When the butler announced that dinner was served, the lady of the house led the company into the dining room and invited them to sit at assigned seats. She encouraged the guests to serve themselves from the dish in front of them and then pass their plates around the table in order to partake of the other fare.

The recipes that follow include both hot and cold dishes from Colonial Williamsburg's taverns inspired by old recipes from eighteenth-century Virginia.

PREVIOUS PAGES: Shrimp Marinated in Fresh Dill, left, and assorted appetizers, right.

Cheese Wafers

MAKES 36 WAFERS

*These wafers will last for several weeks if kept tightly covered
in a tin and stored in a cool, dry place.*

1 cup flour, plus more for kneading
1 teaspoon salt
½ teaspoon ground ginger
⅓ cup chilled vegetable shortening

1 cup grated sharp cheese, such as
  Cheddar, tightly packed
¼ cup toasted sesame seeds
½ teaspoon Worcestershire sauce
2–3 tablespoons ice water

In the bowl of a food processor, combine the flour, salt, ginger, shortening, cheese, sesame seeds, and Worcestershire sauce. Process in several quick, short pulses until blended. With the blades in motion, pour in just enough ice water to make a soft dough that forms a ball around the blades. Turn out onto a floured work surface and knead briefly. Divide the dough in half, making 2 logs 8 inches long and 1¼ inches in diameter. Chill for 20 minutes or until firm.

Preheat the oven to 400°F. and grease 2 large baking sheets. Slice the logs into ⅛-inch-thick wafers and place on the baking sheets. Prick with a fork and bake until lightly browned, 10–12 minutes. Cool on a wire rack.

> SESAME SEEDS ADD A NUTTY FLAVOR TO CHEESE WAFERS. KNOWN IN AFRICA AS "BENNE" OR "BENNI," THE SEEDS WERE BROUGHT TO AMERICA ON SLAVE SHIPS AND SOON BECAME POPULAR IN SOUTHERN COOKING.

Melon Balls with Virginia Ham

MAKES 24–36 PIECES

6–8 ounces Virginia ham, very thinly
  sliced

1 honeydew or cantaloupe
Toothpicks or small skewers

Trim the ham into strips that measure 1 inch wide × 4 inches long. Halve the melon and remove all seeds. Use a melon ball tool to form 1-inch-round balls. Drain on paper towels.

Wrap each melon ball with a strip of ham and secure with a toothpick or small skewer. Chill well before serving.

Virginia Ham Biscuits

MAKES 40 REGULAR OR 70 COCKTAIL BISCUITS

1 recipe Mrs. Booth's Biscuit Mix
  (page 158)
Milk as needed, 3–4 tablespoons per cup
  of mix
Flour for kneading

Melted unsalted butter or milk for
  brushing
1¼–1½ pounds Virginia ham, very
  thinly sliced

Preheat the oven to 425°F. and grease 2 large baking sheets.

In a large bowl, place the biscuit mix. Using a fork, stir in enough milk to make a soft but not sticky dough, 3–4 tablespoons per cup of mix. Knead on a lightly floured work surface until the dough is smooth and elastic.

Roll the dough out ¼-inch thick, then fold over so that the biscuits will open easily when baked. Cut with a 1½–2-inch biscuit cutter (or smaller for cocktail size) and place on the baking sheets. Brush the tops with melted butter or milk. Bake for 7–10 minutes, or until golden brown. Open the biscuits and place pieces of ham inside. Serve warm.

Chowning's Tavern Crabmeat and Artichoke Casserole

SERVES 6–8

For an amusing presentation, cook and serve this recipe in crab-shaped containers that can be found in specialty kitchen equipment stores.

1 pound flaked crabmeat (about 3 cups)
8 artichoke hearts, boiled until tender and chokes removed, or 2 (9-ounce) packages frozen artichoke hearts, thawed
1 small onion, finely chopped
½ green bell pepper, finely chopped
1 tablespoon lemon juice
Salt and freshly ground black pepper to taste

3 tablespoons unsalted butter
3 tablespoons flour
2 cups Chicken Stock (recipe follows) or low-salt canned chicken stock
1 cup fresh bread crumbs
½ cup grated Parmesan cheese
2 tablespoons (¼ stick) unsalted butter, melted

Pick over the crab to remove any bits of broken shell. Pat the artichokes dry with paper towels and cut into ½-inch pieces.

In a large bowl, mix together the crab, artichokes, onion, green pepper, and lemon juice. Season with salt and pepper and transfer to a buttered 2-quart baking dish.

In a medium saucepan over medium heat, melt the 3 tablespoons butter. Add the flour and stir until well blended and lemon colored, about 3 minutes. Pour in the chicken stock, increase the heat to high, and bring to a boil, stirring often. Reduce the heat to medium and simmer until thick and smooth, about 10 minutes. Season with salt and pepper. Cool slightly and pour over the crab mixture. The casserole can be prepared to this point up to a day in advance. Keep covered and refrigerated until ready to bake.

Preheat the oven to 350°F. In a small bowl, mix the bread crumbs with the cheese. Sprinkle over the top of the baking dish and drizzle with the melted butter. Bake until browned on top and bubbling hot, 25–30 minutes.

Chicken Stock

MAKES 4 QUARTS

Several sprigs thyme
Several sprigs parsley
1 bay leaf
1 teaspoon whole black peppercorns
3 celery ribs, coarsely chopped

3 carrots, coarsely chopped
2 onions, sliced
2 leeks, white part only, thickly sliced
5 chicken necks, backs, and wings
Salt to taste

Tie the thyme, parsley, bay leaf, and peppercorns in a large square of cheesecloth. Place in a large soup pot or kettle. Add the celery, carrots, onions, leeks, and chicken parts. Pour in enough cold water to cover. Bring to a boil over high heat, reduce the heat to medium low, and simmer, partially covered, for 2–3 hours. Occasionally skim off any scum that rises to the top. Remove the chicken. Return the stock to the heat and simmer, uncovered, until the stock is reduced to 4 quarts. Season with salt, cool to room temperature, then refrigerate.

Shrimp Marinated in Fresh Dill

SERVES 8–10

FOR THE SHRIMP
1 tablespoon salt
1 teaspoon chopped fresh dill weed
1 lemon, sliced
2½ pounds medium shrimp in shells

FOR THE MARINADE
½ cup olive oil
½ cup dry white wine
1 tablespoon chopped fresh dill weed
1 teaspoon freshly ground black pepper
2 drops Tabasco sauce
½ cup lemon juice
Salt to taste
1 tablespoon snipped chives

In a large pot, combine 1 quart water, the salt, dill weed, and lemon and bring to a boil over high heat. Add the shrimp, reduce the heat to medium, and cook until the shrimp are firm and pink, 3–4 minutes. Drain immediately and chill. Peel and devein the shrimp and place in a crock or bowl.

In a small bowl, mix the oil, wine, dill, pepper, Tabasco, lemon juice, salt, and chives. Pour over the shrimp. Chill at least 2 hours before serving.

Smoked Trout with Horseradish Sauce

SERVES 4

FOR THE HORSERADISH SAUCE
1 cup mayonnaise
¼ cup sour cream
1 tablespoon drained bottled
  horseradish or more to taste
1 tablespoon capers, drained and
  coarsely chopped
1 teaspoon lemon juice
Salt and freshly ground black pepper

FOR THE SMOKED TROUT
4 smoked trout fillets (5 ounces each)
Several large Boston lettuce leaves,
  washed and trimmed
½ small red onion, finely diced
1 lemon, cut into wedges
8–10 cherry tomatoes, halved

In a small bowl, combine the mayonnaise, sour cream, horseradish, capers, and lemon juice. Season with salt and pepper, cover, and chill.

Remove all skin and bones from the trout and trim into attractive pieces. Line 4 individual serving plates with the lettuce leaves, place the trout on top, and garnish with the onion, lemon wedges, and tomatoes. Serve with the horseradish sauce.

Meat Patties in Crust

MAKES 24 PATTIES

1 pound frozen puff pastry (2 sheets),
  thawed according to package
  directions
1 cup ground Virginia ham or smoked
  ham
½ pound ground veal or beef, cooked
  and drained

1 tablespoon chopped fresh parsley
½ teaspoon chopped fresh thyme leaves
  or ¼ teaspoon dried thyme
1 teaspoon grated nutmeg
½ teaspoon freshly ground black pepper

Preheat the oven to 350°F. Roll the pastry into thin sheets and cut into twenty-four 3-inch squares. In a large bowl, mix together the ham, veal or beef, parsley, thyme, nutmeg, and pepper. Place 1 tablespoon of the meat mixture onto each square. Fold the squares in half to form triangles and press the edges together firmly. Place on an ungreased baking sheet and bake for 15–20 minutes, or until golden brown. Serve warm.

Soups

E IGHTEENTH-CENTURY English cookbook author Hannah Glasse gave explicit instructions for making soup: "First take great care the pots or saucepans and covers be very clean and free from all grease and sand, and that they be well tinned, for fear of giving the broths or soups any brassy taste." She favored cooking soups gently, and warned her readers not to "put much more water than you intend to have soup or broth."

Soup was the mainstay of the diet of everyone in the colony of Virginia because it was so easy and inexpensive to prepare. Cooked in one pot from whatever was available or from leftovers, soup needed only to be stirred occasionally, thus enabling busy housewives and slave cooks to attend to other tasks. Poor whites and slaves usually ate hominy made from coarsely ground cornmeal boiled in water. The gentry enjoyed hominy porridge for breakfast in the winter, with milk being substituted for water.

The abundance of farm-fresh vegetables, of both freshwater and ocean seafood, and the variety of fowl and meat enlivened the soups offered on tavern menus then and now.

PREVIOUS PAGES: Gingered Pumpkin Soup with Molasses Cream, left, and Beef Tea with Barley Soup, right.

Beef Tea with Barley Soup

SERVES 8–10

2 medium onions, finely chopped
2 medium carrots, peeled and finely
  chopped
2 celery ribs, finely chopped
2 medium plum tomatoes, peeled,
  seeded, and chopped

10 cups Beef Stock (recipe follows) or
  low-salt canned beef stock
6 ounces lean beef, cut into ¼-inch dice
½ cup barley
Salt and freshly ground pepper to taste
1 recipe Sippets (page 164)

In a large saucepan or soup pot over medium-high heat, place the onions, carrots, celery, tomatoes, and beef stock. Bring to a boil, reduce the heat to low, and simmer, partially covered, until the flavors are well blended, about 20 minutes. Skim off any scum that rises to the surface.

Add the beef and barley to the soup and cook until the barley is tender, 20–25 minutes. Season with salt and pepper. Serve with Sippets.

Beef Stock

MAKES 2–3 QUARTS

10 pounds meaty beef bones
2 tablespoons vegetable oil
3 medium onions, coarsely chopped
2 carrots, coarsely chopped
2 celery ribs, coarsely chopped
2 cloves garlic, minced

1 (14½-ounce) can tomatoes, coarsely
  chopped
½ cup tomato puree
Several sprigs thyme
½ teaspoon freshly ground black pepper
1 bay leaf

Preheat the oven to 400°F. In a large roasting pan, place the bones. Pour the oil over and stir in the onions, carrots, and celery. Roast, stirring often, until well browned, about 35–45 minutes. Drain off all fat.

In a large soup pot or kettle, place the bones and all vegetables. Add the garlic, tomatoes, tomato puree, thyme, pepper, and bay leaf. Pour in enough cold water to cover. Bring to a boil over high heat and skim off any scum that rises to the surface. Reduce the heat to low and simmer, uncovered, skimming often, until the liquid has reduced and the flavor is rich, 6–8 hours. Strain the stock through a double thickness of cheesecloth. Cool to room temperature. Refrigerate overnight. Skim.

Eastern Shore Clam Chowder

SERVES 8–10

The word "chowder" comes from the French chaudière, *a large iron cooking pot traditionally used for making stews. Filled with chewy bits of tasty clams and a touch of salty pork, clam chowder is a Virginia favorite. For a quicker and easier version of the following recipe, use two 8-ounce bottles clam juice and two 6½-ounce cans minced clams in place of fresh clams.*

12 large clams
¼ pound slab bacon or salt pork, cut
   into ¼-inch cubes
2 medium onions, finely chopped
3 medium all-purpose potatoes, peeled
   and cut into ½-inch dice

2 tablespoons cornmeal or flour
1 cup light cream or half-and-half
Salt and freshly ground white pepper to
   taste

Scrub the clams. In a large pot, place the clams in enough water to cover. Cover and bring to a boil. Cook until they are open, about 5 minutes. Remove the clams from their shells, chop finely, and reserve. Strain the liquid and add enough water to make 6 cups.

In a large saucepan, place the bacon or salt pork. Cook over medium-high heat, stirring often, until crisp and brown. Add the onions, potatoes, chopped clams, and the 6 cups liquid. Bring to a simmer and cook until the potatoes are tender, about 20 minutes.

In a small bowl, mix the cornmeal or flour with a little cold water. Stir into the chowder and add the cream. Season with salt and pepper. Serve in warmed bowls.

Corn Chowder

SERVES 6

The cream-style corn called for here comes in a can. Make your own by cooking
fresh kernels in butter and pulsing briefly in a food processor.

3 ounces salt pork, cut into small cubes
1 large onion, finely chopped
1 celery rib, chopped
2 medium all-purpose potatoes, peeled
  and cut into ½-inch dice
2 cups Chicken Stock (page 24) or
  low-salt canned chicken stock

2 cups cream-style corn
2 cups milk
¼ cup (½ stick) unsalted butter
Salt and freshly ground white pepper to
  taste

In a large heavy saucepan, place the salt pork. Cook over medium-high heat, stirring
often, until lightly browned and the fat has rendered, 3–5 minutes. Add the onion and
cook, stirring often, until softened, about 5 minutes. Add the celery, potatoes, chicken
stock, and 1 cup water. Cook until the potatoes are tender, 15–20 minutes. Stir in the
corn and cook 5 minutes longer.

In a small saucepan over medium-high heat, heat the milk and butter until the butter has melted. Stir this mixture into the chowder and season with salt and pepper.
Serve hot.

She-Crab Soup

*She-crab roe gives a distinctive flavor to this soup. Harvesting female crabs
has been restricted recently in order to replenish dwindling stocks.
The flying fish roe replaces the traditional female crab roe.*

12 live blue crabs (about ½ pound each)
3 tablespoons unsalted butter
4 tablespoons flour
3 cups milk
1 cup heavy cream
1 teaspoon finely grated lemon peel
¼ teaspoon paprika

Dash cayenne pepper
Salt and freshly ground white pepper to
  taste
¼ cup dry sherry
2–3 tablespoons flying fish roe (available
  in Asian markets), for garnish

Bring a large pot of salted water to a boil over high heat. Add the crabs and return to
a boil. Reduce the heat to low and simmer, tightly covered, for 15 minutes. Drain,
transfer the cooked crabs to a bowl, and cool.

In a large heavy saucepan over medium-low heat, melt the butter. Add the flour
and cook, whisking constantly, until lemon colored, about 3 minutes. Pour in the milk
and cream. Reduce the heat to medium low and simmer, stirring often, until smooth
and thick. Do not boil.

Remove the meat and any roe from the crabs. Discard the shells. Add the crabmeat, any crab roe, lemon peel, paprika, cayenne, and salt and pepper and heat
through. Stir in the sherry just before serving. Garnish with the flying fish roe and
serve at once.

Shields Tavern Crayfish Soup

SERVES 8–10

Crayfish is an edible freshwater crustacean similar in taste and structure to lobster. The crawfish, or crawdad, as it is also known, is found in ponds and streams throughout the country. This flavorful soup is a signature dish in Williamsburg taverns.

1 (14-ounce) can clam juice
½ cube fish bouillon
1 pound shelled crayfish tails (thawed if frozen), coarsely chopped
½ cup (1 stick) unsalted butter
1 small onion, finely chopped
½ celery rib, finely chopped
1 small clove garlic, minced
1 cup flour
½ cup heavy cream

1 teaspoon chopped fresh thyme or ½ teaspoon dried thyme
Dash Tabasco sauce
Dash Worcestershire sauce
¼ teaspoon bottled Creole seasoning mix
Salt and freshly ground black pepper to taste
1 tablespoon dry sherry

In a large heavy saucepan, combine 6 cups water, the clam juice, and bouillon cube. Bring to a boil over high heat, add the crayfish, and bring back to a boil. Drain immediately, reserving the liquid. Transfer the blanched crayfish to a bowl, cover, and refrigerate until ready to serve.

In a medium heavy saucepan over medium-high heat, melt the butter. Add the onion and celery. Cook, stirring often, until softened, 3–5 minutes. Add the garlic and cook 1 minute longer. Add the flour and cook, stirring often, until the mixture is lemon colored, 2–3 minutes. Pour in the liquid used to blanch the crayfish and increase the heat to high. Bring to a boil, whisking constantly. Reduce the heat to medium low and pour in the cream. Simmer, partially covered, until the soup is thickened and smooth, about 30 minutes.

Add the reserved crayfish and season the soup with the thyme, Tabasco sauce, Worcestershire sauce, Creole seasoning, and salt and pepper. Cook 3–5 minutes longer to blend the flavors and heat through the crayfish. Stir the sherry into the soup just before serving.

King's Arms Tavern Cream of Peanut Soup

SERVES 10–12

Columbus took peanuts, native to South America, back to Europe, then Portuguese slave traders introduced them to Africa. The legumes recrossed the Atlantic on slave ships. The peanut soup now served at the King's Arms Tavern is a variation of a recipe developed by George Washington Carver in the early 1900s.

¼ cup (½ stick) unsalted butter
1 medium onion, finely chopped
2 celery ribs, finely chopped
3 tablespoons flour
8 cups Chicken Stock (page 24) or
 low-salt canned chicken stock

2 cups smooth peanut butter
1¾ cups light cream or half-and-half
Finely chopped salted peanuts, for
 garnish

In a large saucepan or soup pot over medium heat, melt the butter. Add the onion and celery and cook, stirring often, until softened, 3–5 minutes. Stir in the flour and cook 2 minutes longer. Pour in the chicken stock, increase the heat to high, and bring to a boil, stirring constantly. Reduce the heat to medium and cook, stirring often, until slightly reduced and thickened, about 15 minutes. Pour into a sieve set over a large bowl and strain, pushing hard on the solids to extract as much flavor as possible. Return the liquid to the saucepan or pot.

Whisk the peanut butter and the cream into the liquid. Warm over low heat, whisking often, for about 5 minutes, or until hot. Do not boil. Serve warm, garnished with the chopped peanuts.

Cream of Watercress Soup

SERVES 6

Watercress grows wild in streams around Williamsburg. The small leaves have a slight peppery taste that makes a flavorful soup.

1 bunch watercress
2 tablespoons (¼ stick) unsalted butter
2 medium all-purpose potatoes, peeled and thinly sliced
1 large leek, white part only, cleaned and thinly sliced

2 cups Chicken Stock (page 24) or low-salt canned chicken stock
2 cups milk
1 cup heavy cream
Salt and freshly ground black pepper to taste

Remove the large bitter stems of the watercress and wash the leaves in several changes of cold water. Reserve several of the nicest leaves for garnish. Coarsely chop the rest.

In a large heavy saucepan over medium-high heat, melt the butter. Add the chopped watercress, potatoes, leek, and ¼ cup water. Reduce the heat to low and simmer, covered, until the potatoes are very tender, about 20 minutes. Pour in the chicken stock and milk. Increase the heat to high and bring to a boil. Reduce the heat to low, cover, and cook 20 minutes longer.

Transfer the soup to a food processor or blender and blend until smooth, in batches if necessary. Return the soup to the saucepan and place over low heat. Pour in the cream and cook, stirring often, until hot. Do not boil. Season with salt and pepper. Serve hot, garnished with the reserved watercress leaves.

Chesapeake Oyster Bisque

SERVES 8–10

The bays, estuaries, and tidal creeks of Chesapeake Bay have long been home to the delicious Chesapeake oyster. Colonists were amazed at the abundance of oysters, which were expensive delicacies in Europe. These bivalves were often made into stews and soups similar to this bisque.

1 quart shucked oysters with their liquor
1 bay leaf
2 medium onions, finely chopped
2 celery ribs, finely chopped
½ cup (1 stick) unsalted butter
¼ cup flour

½ teaspoon salt
¼ teaspoon freshly ground white pepper
2 cups light cream or half-and-half
¼ cup dry sherry
Paprika, for garnish
Finely chopped parsley, for garnish

In a strainer set over a bowl, place the oysters and drain, reserving all the liquor. Remove the oysters from the strainer, coarsely chop, cover, and refrigerate until just before serving.

Measure the reserved liquor and add enough cold water to make 4 cups. Into a small heavy saucepan, pour the liquid. Add the bay leaf, half the onions, and half the celery. Simmer, uncovered, for 30 minutes, then strain.

In a separate heavy saucepan over medium-high heat, melt the butter. Add the remaining onions and celery. Cook, stirring often, until softened, about 5 minutes. Stir in the flour and cook 3 minutes longer. Pour in the strained broth, increase the heat to high, and bring to a boil, whisking constantly. Season with the salt and pepper, reduce the heat to medium low, and simmer until thickened, 7–10 minutes. Add the chopped oysters and stir in the cream. Cook just until heated through, 2–3 minutes. Do not boil.

Stir in the sherry just before serving. Ladle the bisque into warmed bowls, sprinkle with paprika and parsley, and serve.

Gingered Pumpkin Soup with Molasses Cream

SERVES 8–10

FOR THE SOUP
2 tablespoons (¼ stick) unsalted butter
1 small onion, finely chopped
1 celery rib, finely chopped
2 cups cooked fresh pumpkin puree, or
  2 (16-ounce) cans unsweetened puree
4 cups Chicken Stock (page 24) or
  low-salt canned chicken stock
2 cups light cream or half-and-half

1 tablespoon sugar
½ teaspoon ground ginger
Salt and freshly ground black pepper to
  taste

FOR THE MOLASSES CREAM
1 cup heavy cream
2 tablespoons dark molasses

To prepare the soup, in a large heavy saucepan over medium-high heat, melt the butter. Add the onion and celery and cook, stirring often, until tender, 3–5 minutes. Stir in the pumpkin and chicken stock. Increase the heat to high and bring to a boil, stirring often.

Reduce the heat to low and pour in the cream. Stir in the sugar and ginger. Season with salt and pepper and heat until warmed through, about 5 minutes. Do not boil.

To make the garnish, in a large bowl, combine the cream and molasses. Beat with an electric mixer until the cream forms soft peaks.

MOLASSES IS A KISSING COUSIN OF TREACLE, WHICH BRITONS CALL THE DARK BROWN OR BLACK SWEET SYRUPS OBTAINED DURING THE SUGAR REFINING PROCESS.

Ladle the soup into warmed bowls. Garnish with a dollop of the cream and serve any remaining cream on the side.

Vegetable Gumbo with Rice

SERVES 10–12

*Gumbo is a uniquely American dish with a strong southern history. It has long been
popular throughout the region. "Gumbo" is a traditional African word for the okra plant,
an essential ingredient in all variations.*

¼ cup (½ stick) unsalted butter
2 medium onions, finely chopped
1 large celery rib, thinly sliced
1 small green bell pepper, cored and
  finely chopped
1 clove garlic, minced
2 tablespoons flour
4 cups Chicken Stock (page 24) or
  low-salt canned chicken stock
4–5 large tomatoes, peeled, seeded, and
  chopped, or 2 (16-ounce) cans,
  drained, seeded, and chopped

1 teaspoon chopped fresh thyme or
  ½ teaspoon dried thyme
2 teaspoons salt
½ teaspoon freshly ground black pepper
¼ teaspoon cayenne pepper
1 pound fresh or frozen okra, trimmed
  and sliced
2 cups hot cooked rice
Finely chopped fresh parsley, for garnish

In a large pot or casserole over medium-high heat, melt the butter. Add the onions,
celery, and green pepper. Cook, stirring often, until softened, 3–5 minutes. Add the
garlic and cook 1 minute longer. Stir in the flour and cook, stirring constantly, until
well blended, about 2 minutes. Pour in the chicken stock and increase the heat to high.
Bring to a boil, stirring often.

Reduce the heat to medium low and add the tomatoes, thyme, salt, black pepper,
and cayenne pepper. Simmer, partially covered, for 30 minutes, or until slightly thickened and the flavors have blended.

Add the okra to the gumbo about 10 minutes before serving. Divide the rice
among 10–12 warmed soup bowls and ladle the gumbo on top. Sprinkle with a pinch
of parsley and serve at once.

White Bean Soup

SERVES 8–10

Garnish this soup with garlicky croutons made with day-old French bread. Half of the cooked beans are pureed to thicken the soup and the rest are left chunky for texture.

2 cups dried white navy beans (about 1 pound)
2 tablespoons vegetable oil
1 large onion, finely chopped
1 celery rib, finely chopped

1 clove garlic, minced
1 meaty ham hock (about 1 pound)
¼ cup chopped fresh parsley
Salt and freshly ground black pepper to taste

Rinse the beans in a colander under cold running water. In a large bowl, place the beans and pour in enough cold water to cover. Soak overnight. Rinse again under cold water and drain well.

In a large soup pot over medium-high heat, heat the oil. Add the onion and celery. Cook, stirring often, until softened, 3–5 minutes. Add the garlic and cook 1 minute longer. Stir in the drained beans and add the ham hock. Pour in 4 quarts cold water and bring to a boil over high heat. Reduce the heat to medium low and cook, partially covered, until the beans are very soft, about 3 hours.

Remove the ham hock to a bowl and cool. Puree half the soup in a food processor. Return the puree to the soup and season with salt and pepper.

When the ham hock is cool enough to handle, discard all skin, fat, and gristle. Remove the meat from the bone and cut into ½-inch pieces. Add the ham to the soup. Stir in the parsley and season with salt and pepper. (If the soup is too thin, bring to a boil and cook, uncovered, over high heat for about 10 minutes to thicken.) Serve at once in warmed bowls.

Yellow Split Pea and Sausage Soup

SERVES 6–8

*Omit the sausages for a lighter soup. A peeled, seeded, and
chopped tomato may be added for color.*

2 cups dried yellow split peas (about 1
    pound), washed and picked over
1 meaty ham hock (about 1 pound)
2 medium onions, finely chopped
1 celery rib, finely chopped

4 Surry or other smoked sausages
Salt and freshly ground black pepper to
    taste
Finely chopped fresh parsley, for garnish

In a large saucepan or soup pot, place the peas and add the ham hock, onions, and
celery. Pour in enough cold water to cover, about 2 quarts. Bring to a boil over high
heat, reduce the heat to low, and simmer, partially covered, until the peas are very soft,
about 1¼ hours.

Remove the ham hock to a bowl and cool. When cool enough to handle, discard
all skin, fat, and gristle. Remove the meat from the bone and cut into ½-inch pieces.
Working in batches, puree the soup into a food processor until smooth. Return the
puree to the saucepan or pot, stir in the pieces of ham, cover, and keep warm over
low heat.

Place the sausages in a skillet large enough to hold them in a flat layer. Add ½ cup
water, cover, and cook over medium-low heat until plumped and the juices run clear
when pricked with a fork, about 10 minutes. Pour off all the liquid from the skillet and
cook the sausages, turning constantly, until browned, 3–5 minutes. Drain on paper
towels. Cut into ¼-inch-thick slices.

Season the soup with salt and pepper and ladle into warmed bowls. Garnish with
slices of sausage and a pinch of parsley. Serve at once.

Salads, Dressings, Relishes, and Condiments

EAGER for fresh salads, Virginia settlers hastened to pick the first spring lettuces from their gardens or to gather wild greens from the meadows or streams. Avid gardeners both, Thomas Jefferson and his Williamsburg cousin John Randolph noted that they harvested a variety of salad greens and herbs in the spring and fall. When warm summer weather caused the greens to bolt, salads generally consisted of cucumbers and onions.

Mary Randolph's instructions for preparing salad greens are as appropriate today as they were in 1824: "To have this delicate dish in perfection, the lettuce, pepper grass, chervil, cress, &c. should be gathered early in the morning, nicely picked, washed, and laid in cold water, which will be improved by adding ice; just before dinner is ready to be served, drain the water from your salad, cut it into a bowl, giving the proper proportions of each plant."

In the fall, Virginia housewives prepared zesty pickles, relishes, and condiments to whet appetites they knew would tire of a diet of root vegetables long before spring greens became available. Sweet and sour accompaniments were always welcome beside the main dish.

Cookbook writers gave precise instructions for pickling. "Always use Stone Jars for all Sorts of Pickles . . . be sure never to put your Hands in to take Pickles out, it will soon spoil it [the pickling mixture]. The best Way is to every Pot, tye a wooden Spoon full of little Holes, to take the Pickles out with," Hannah Glasse admonished.

These tasty condiments are as popular with today's tavern diners as they were two hundred years ago. Colorful, spicy, and easy to put together, they are sure to be relished by all.

Christiana Campbell's Tavern Crabmeat Salad

SERVES 4

Serve this delicate salad very well chilled with wedges of fresh tomatoes and ripe avocados.

1 pound backfin crabmeat (about
  3 cups)
2 celery ribs, peeled and finely chopped
½ cup mayonnaise
1 tablespoon lemon juice
Salt and freshly ground white pepper to
  taste

Dash Tabasco sauce
2 tablespoons Vinaigrette Dressing
  (recipe follows)
Several large lettuce leaves, washed and
  trimmed
1 recipe Johnnycakes (page 160)

Pick over the crabmeat and remove any bits of shell. In a large bowl, combine the crabmeat and celery.

In a small bowl, combine the mayonnaise, lemon juice, salt and pepper, Tabasco sauce, and vinaigrette dressing. Blend well and pour over the crabmeat mixture. Fold gently to mix without shredding the crabmeat. Cover and chill at least 2 hours.

Line a chilled platter or individual plates with lettuce leaves. Mound the salad in the center and serve at once with Johnnycakes.

Vinaigrette Dressing

MAKES ¾ CUP

*Serve this versatile dressing with seasonal vegetables, fresh salad greens,
or cold meats or poultry.*

¾ teaspoon dry mustard
¼ cup red or white wine vinegar
1 teaspoon salt

½ teaspoon freshly ground black pepper
6 tablespoons vegetable oil
6 tablespoons olive oil

In a small bowl, whisk together the mustard, vinegar, salt, and pepper to dissolve the salt. Slowly pour in the vegetable and olive oils, whisking constantly, until the dressing is thick and emulsified. Keep covered in the refrigerator until ready to serve.

Boston Lettuce and Arugula Salad
with Fresh Oranges and Walnut Dressing

*Tangerines or blood oranges are an exotic substitution for the
oranges in this innovative salad. Use small leaves of arugula for best results.
Bitter larger leaves tend to overwhelm the citrus flavor.*

2 small heads Boston lettuce, cored,
  trimmed, and washed
4 cups loosely packed arugula, large
  stems removed and leaves washed

3 medium oranges
¾ cup lightly toasted walnuts, broken
  into large pieces
1 recipe Walnut Dressing (recipe follows)

Arrange the Boston lettuce leaves flat on 8 chilled salad plates. In a large bowl, place
the arugula.

Cut away the peel, pith, and skin of the oranges. Remove whole sections by sliding
a knife down one side of a segment and cutting it from the membrane. Cut down the
other side and pull out the sections.

Add the orange sections and walnuts to the arugula. Pour the walnut dressing over
the salad just before serving.

Arrange the salad on top of the plates lined with lettuce leaves. Drizzle over any
dressing left in the bottom of the bowl. Serve at once.

Walnut Dressing

½ teaspoon Dijon mustard
3 tablespoons red wine vinegar
½ teaspoon salt

¼ teaspoon freshly ground black pepper
¼ cup vegetable oil
¼ cup walnut oil

In a small bowl, combine the mustard, vinegar, and salt and pepper. Add the vegetable and walnut oils in a slow, steady stream, whisking constantly, until blended.

Shields Tavern Salmagundi

SERVES 8

Recipes for Salmagundi abound in eighteenth-century cookbooks. Hannah Glasse in her 1747 book The Art of Cookery Made Plain and Easy *suggested garnishing it with "stertion" [nasturtium] flowers, a once-thought-exotic ingredient. This version of the modern chef's salad was often made with leftovers and served for supper, a lighter meal than dinner.*

10 cups loosely packed assorted salad
  greens (Boston lettuce, romaine,
  endive, leaf lettuce, radicchio, or
  chicory), washed and trimmed
1 recipe Vinaigrette Dressing (page 45)
1 pound thinly sliced Virginia ham, cut
  into strips
1 pound thinly sliced turkey or chicken,
  cut into strips

1 pound sliced Cheddar cheese, cut into
  strips
4 hard-cooked eggs, sliced
8 celery ribs, peeled and cut into long
  sticks
16 black olives, pitted
16 anchovy fillets, drained and rinsed if
  canned

Toss the salad greens with enough of the vinaigrette dressing to coat. Arrange the dressed greens on a large platter and garnish with the ham, turkey, Cheddar cheese, eggs, celery, olives, and anchovies. Serve any remaining dressing on the side.

OPPOSITE: *King's Arms Tavern Spinach Salad with Smithfield Ham Lardoons and Chutney Dressing,* top, *and Boston Lettuce and Arugula Salad with Fresh Oranges and Walnut Dressing,* bottom.

Celery Root Slaw

SERVES 4–6

Celery root is a hearty late fall or early winter vegetable that makes an unusual and delicious slaw. Have a cut lemon handy when stacking and cutting the root. Rub the exposed surfaces of the peeled root with the lemon to keep it from turning dark.

1 medium celery root (celeriac), about 1 pound
1 medium carrot
1 small onion

1 recipe Buttermilk Chiffon Dressing (recipe follows)
Salt and freshly ground black pepper to taste

Peel the celery root and cut into thin slices. Stack the slices and cut them lengthwise into julienne strips. (Alternatively, use a rotary shredder or food processor with a shredding attachment.) Transfer the strips to a bowl of ice water to prevent discoloration.

Peel the carrot and cut into thin julienne slices. Peel the onion, cut crosswise into ⅛-inch-thick slices, and separate into rings.

Just before serving, drain the celery root and pat dry with paper towels. In a large bowl, toss the celery root, carrot, and onion with enough of the dressing to coat thoroughly. Season with salt and pepper. Cover and refrigerate for 2–3 hours. Serve cold with any remaining dressing on the side.

Buttermilk Chiffon Dressing

MAKES 1½ CUPS

Tangy buttermilk gives this dressing a delightful twist.

¼ cup white wine vinegar
1 tablespoon sugar
¼ teaspoon paprika
1 teaspoon salt

½ teaspoon freshly ground black pepper
⅔ cup vegetable oil
¼ cup sour cream
¼ cup buttermilk

In a small bowl, combine the vinegar, sugar, paprika, salt, and pepper. Whisk to dissolve the sugar and salt. Add the vegetable oil in a slow, steady stream, whisking constantly, until thick and smooth. Stir in the sour cream and buttermilk. Chill thoroughly before serving.

King's Arms Tavern Spinach Salad
with Smithfield Ham Lardoons and Chutney Dressing

SERVES 4–6

*The earthy spinach marries well with the sweet chutney and smoky ham
in this recipe. Serve with sliced ripe tomatoes and crusty bread.*

¼ pound country ham or Smithfield
   ham
1 tablespoon vegetable oil

1 pound tender young spinach leaves,
   washed and large stems removed
1 recipe King's Arms Tavern Chutney
   Dressing (recipe follows)

Cut the ham into ¼-inch-thick slices. Stack 2 slices on top of each other and cut crosswise into ¼-inch strips to form lardoons. Continue with the rest of the ham.

In a small skillet over medium heat, heat the oil. Add the lardoons and cook, stirring often, until lightly browned and crisp, 3–5 minutes. Drain well on paper towels.

In a large bowl, place the spinach and sprinkle the lardoons over. Toss with just
enough of the chutney dressing to moisten and flavor the salad. Serve the remaining
dressing on the side.

King's Arms Tavern Chutney Dressing

MAKES 1 ½ CUPS

Store-bought bottled chutney makes this an easy-to-prepare and unusual salad dressing.

½ cup red wine vinegar
¼ teaspoon dry mustard
½ teaspoon salt
¼ teaspoon freshly ground white pepper

¼ cup Mango Chutney (page 54) or
   bottled Major Grey's Chutney, finely
   chopped
¾ cup vegetable oil

In a small bowl, whisk together the vinegar, mustard, salt, and pepper to dissolve the
salt. Stir in the chutney. Add the oil in a slow, steady stream, whisking constantly, until
the dressing is thick and emulsified. The dressing keeps, tightly covered, in the refrigerator for up to 1 week.

Christiana Campbell's Tavern Slaw

SERVES 8

*The early colonists found that English cabbage plants grew year-round
in the mild Tidewater climate.*

1 white or green cabbage (about 1½
  pounds), halved and cored
1 celery rib, thinly sliced
1 small onion, halved and thinly sliced
½ red bell pepper, cut into ¼-inch dice
1 cup mayonnaise

1 teaspoon red wine vinegar
1 teaspoon Dijon mustard
1 teaspoon celery seed
Salt and freshly ground black pepper to
  taste

Finely shred or grate the cabbage. In a large bowl, place the cabbage and add the celery, onion, and red pepper. In a small bowl, mix together the mayonnaise, vinegar, mustard, celery seed, and salt and pepper. Pour over the cabbage mixture and toss well. Cover and refrigerate for 2–3 hours before serving.

Salads, Dressings, Relishes, and Condiments

Sweet Potato Salad

Check the potatoes often while cooking. Remove and drain as soon as they are tender.
If cooked too long, they become so soft that it is difficult to toss them
without turning the potatoes into a puree.

2–3 medium sweet potatoes (about
  2 pounds), peeled and cut into ½-inch
  cubes
1 tablespoon lemon juice
1 celery rib, thinly sliced
1 small Golden Delicious apple, peeled,
  cored, and cut into ¼-inch dice

3 medium oranges
¼ cup coarsely chopped pecans
1 cup mayonnaise
Salt and freshly ground black pepper to
  taste
Several large Boston lettuce leaves,
  washed and trimmed

In a small saucepan, place the potatoes and enough salted water to cover. Bring to a
boil over high heat, reduce to medium, and simmer until tender but not mushy, about
10 minutes. Drain and toss with lemon juice to prevent discoloration. Cool.

In a large bowl, combine the celery and apple. Cut away the peel, pith, and skin of
the oranges. Remove sections by sliding a knife down each side of a segment and cutting it from the membrane. Pull out the sections, remove any seeds, and add the sections to the celery and apple mixture. Stir in the pecans and mayonnaise.

Just before serving, gently fold in the sweet potatoes, being careful not to crush the
fragile cubes. Season with salt and pepper and serve on lettuce leaves.

Watercress and Artichoke Hearts Salad

SERVES 4–6

4 artichoke hearts, boiled or steamed
   until tender and chokes removed,
   retaining 20 large leaves or
1 (10-ounce) can artichoke hearts,
   or 1 (9-ounce) package frozen
   artichoke hearts, cooked according
   to package directions and cooled

1 bunch watercress, washed and
   trimmed of large stems
½ teaspoon finely grated lemon peel
2 tablespoons lemon juice
½ teaspoon sugar
½ teaspoon salt
⅛ teaspoon freshly ground white pepper
½ cup olive oil

Pat the artichoke hearts dry with paper towels and cut into 1-inch pieces. Place in a large bowl and add the watercress.

In a small bowl, whisk together the lemon peel, lemon juice, sugar, salt, and pepper to dissolve the salt and sugar. Add the olive oil in a slow, steady stream, whisking constantly until blended.

Pour the dressing over the salad just before serving. Toss well. If using fresh artichokes, arrange 5 leaves on each plate. Top with the artichoke mixture. Serve at once.

King's Arms Tavern Dressing

MAKES 3 CUPS

Fresh herbs grow all summer behind the tavern. The chefs use what is most abundant and at peak flavor to make this delicious dressing.

1½ teaspoons Dijon mustard
¾ cup cider vinegar
1½ teaspoons salt
½ teaspoon freshly ground black pepper
1¼ cups vegetable oil

¾ cup olive oil
1 clove garlic, minced
½ teaspoon chopped fresh oregano
½ teaspoon chopped fresh tarragon
2 large basil leaves, finely chopped

In a small bowl, combine the mustard, vinegar, salt, and pepper, whisking to dissolve the salt. Gradually pour in the oils, whisking constantly, until the dressing is thick and emulsified. Stir in the garlic, oregano, tarragon, and basil. Tightly sealed, the dressing keeps in the refrigerator for up to 1 week.

Mango Chutney

MAKES THREE 8-OUNCE JARS

6 mangoes, peeled and sliced
1 pound dates, pitted and diced
2 pounds packed light brown sugar
1 pound seedless raisins
¼ pound crystallized ginger, finely
    chopped

1 clove garlic, minced
¾ teaspoon salt
Cayenne pepper to taste
1 quart cider vinegar

In a large pot, combine the mangoes, dates, sugar, raisins, ginger, garlic, salt, and cayenne. Stir in the vinegar and bring to a boil over high heat. Reduce the heat to medium and simmer, stirring often, until thick, about 30 minutes. Pour into sterilized 8-ounce jars and seal.

"CHUTNEY" COMES FROM THE EAST INDIAN WORD *chatni* AND DESCRIBES A SWEET-AND-SOUR CONDIMENT CONTAINING FRUITS, VEGETABLES, SUGAR, SPICES, AND VINEGAR. CHUTNEYS RANGE IN SPICINESS FROM MILD TO HOT.

CLOCKWISE FROM TOP RIGHT: King's Arms Tavern Ham Relish, Pickled Watermelon Rind, King's Arms Tavern Three-Bean Relish, and Corn Relish.

King's Arms Tavern Three-Bean Relish

SERVES 4–6

1 cup cooked or canned kidney beans,
    drained
1 cup cooked or canned black beans,
    drained
1 cup cooked or frozen and thawed
    black-eyed peas
2 scallions, trimmed and finely
    chopped

1 medium carrot, peeled and cut into
    ¼-inch dice
1 clove garlic, minced
½ cup red wine vinegar
2 tablespoons olive oil
1 tablespoon chopped fresh parsley
Salt and freshly ground black pepper to
    taste

In a large bowl, combine the kidney beans, black beans, and black-eyed peas. Add the scallions, carrot, and garlic. In a small bowl, mix the vinegar with the olive oil until blended. Pour over the beans and stir well. Stir in the parsley and season well with salt and pepper.

Red Pepper Relish

MAKES 1 QUART

1 cup corn syrup
½ cup sugar
¼ cup vinegar
⅛ teaspoon salt

½ teaspoon freshly ground black pepper
¼ teaspoon ground cloves
4 cups cored and diced red bell peppers
1 small onion, finely chopped

In a large saucepan, combine the corn syrup, sugar, vinegar, salt, pepper, and cloves and bring to a boil over high heat. Add the peppers and onion, reduce the heat to medium, and simmer for 15–20 minutes. Cool to room temperature, then cover and chill thoroughly before serving.

Corn Relish

SERVES 4

2 cups cooked corn kernels, thawed if
  frozen
½ cup bottled pickle relish, drained

¼ cup Red Pepper Relish, drained
  (page 55)
Salt and freshly ground black pepper to
  taste

In a small bowl, combine the corn, pickle relish, and red pepper relish. Season with salt and pepper. Drain off any excess liquid before serving.

Cranberry-Orange Relish

MAKES 3 CUPS

2 cups cranberries
1 orange, quartered and seeded
½ lemon, seeded

1 cup sugar
1 cup pecans
¼ cup Cointreau or other orange liqueur

In the bowl of a food processor, combine the cranberries, orange, and lemon and process until coarsely chopped. Add the sugar, pecans, and Cointreau and pulse briefly to mix. Cover and let stand at room temperature for 12 hours. Refrigerate overnight.

King's Arms Tavern Ham Relish

MAKES 6 CUPS

1 large apple, peeled, cored, and
  chopped

4 cups finely chopped Virginia ham
1 cup Red Pepper Relish (page 55)

Place the apple in a small saucepan with 1 tablespoon water. Cook over medium heat until tender but not mushy, about 5 minutes. Cool completely. In a large bowl, combine the ham and pepper relish. Stir in the apple and blend well. Cover and chill well before serving.

Pickled Watermelon Rind

MAKES 4 PINTS

Portuguese traders took watermelons from Africa to Europe before the first English voyages to the New World. Early settlers carried watermelon seeds across the Atlantic. The fruit was growing in Virginia gardens by 1615.

1 large watermelon
½ cup salt
2½ cups cider vinegar
2 cups sugar

1 tablespoon whole cloves
1 tablespoon allspice
2 cinnamon sticks, broken into pieces
4 (1-inch) pieces fresh ginger

Cut the rind from the watermelon, reserving the flesh for another use. Trim off the green skin and cut the rind into 1-inch pieces. (There should be about 8 cups trimmed rind.)

In a large pot, place the rind and pour in enough cold water to cover. Bring to a boil over high heat, then drain at once. Rinse under cold running water and return the rinsed rind to the pot. Repeat this procedure and transfer to a large bowl.

Mix the salt with 6 cups cold water and stir until dissolved. Pour over the rind and let stand for 6–8 hours. Drain in a colander and rinse well under cold running water.

In a large nonreactive saucepan or preserving pan, combine the vinegar and sugar. Pour in 1 cup cold water and stir over medium heat until the sugar has dissolved. Tie the cloves, allspice, cinnamon, and ginger in a square of cheesecloth. Add to the vinegar mixture and increase the heat to high. Bring to a boil and boil for 5 minutes. Add the watermelon rind, reduce the heat to low, and cook until the rind is clear and the syrup is thickened, 45 minutes–1 hour. Remove and discard the bag of spices.

Pack the rind in preserving jars and seal while hot. Cool to room temperature. Store in a dark cool place for 2–3 weeks before serving.

WHETHER WHOLE OR GROUND, CLOVES HAVE BEEN AN IMPORTANT INGREDIENT SINCE ANCIENT TIMES. WHOLE CLOVES ARE A COMMON PICKLING SPICE IN AMERICAN COOKERY AND ARE ALSO USED IN MULLED CIDER AND WINE. GROUND CLOVES APPEAR IN DISHES THAT RANGE FROM STEWS TO SWEETS.

Eggs, Cheese, Vegetarian Dishes, and Savory Pies

"WHEN you buy eggs put the great end to your tongue; if it feels warm, it is new; but if cold it is stale . . . or take the egg, hold it up against the sun or a candle, if the white appears clear and fair, the yolk round it is good; but if muddy or cloudy, and the yolk is broken, it is nought. Or take the egg and put it into a pan of cold water; the fresher it is the sooner it will sink to the bottom." So commented Eliza Smith, author of the English cookbook *The Compleat Housewife.*

Easily cooked–boiled, fried, poached, scrambled–eggs appeared at the dinner table served over toast, as garnishes atop vegetables, and in sweet or savory pies. Although eggs were an everyday food in early America, they were seldom eaten for breakfast until the next century.

Housewives made cream and cottage-type cheeses but the warm climate in Tidewater Virginia is not conducive to curing hard cheeses. Store accounts of imported goods show that Cheshire and Gloucester cheeses came from England. The presence of tin cheese toasters in inventories suggests that some Virginians ate "English rabbit." An eighteenth-century recipe called for pouring a glass of red wine over toasted bread, then covering the toast with thin slices of cheese. "Put it in a tin Oven before the Fire, and it will be toasted and brown presently. Serve it away hot."

Everyone in colonial Virginia ate vegetables and grains, especially corn in the form of hominy. Merchants sold barley, dried split peas, and imported macaroni and vermicelli in the stores along Duke of Gloucester Street. Those who wanted to make pasta themselves found recipes in British cookbooks.

Today, all Colonial Williamsburg taverns prepare vegetarian dishes such as savory pies, baked pasta, and polenta made from finely ground cornmeal for diners who know that meals without meat are deliciously satisfying.

Eggs Benedict with Virginia Ham

SERVES 2

Eggs Benedict made with Sally Lunn are a Williamsburg tradition.
Substitute English muffins, rusks, or thick slices of egg bread if desired.

4 slices Sally Lunn (page 163)
4 thin slices Virginia ham
Salt to taste
4 large eggs

Freshly ground black pepper to taste
1 recipe Hollandaise Sauce (recipe
  follows)

Lightly toast the Sally Lunn and place on warmed serving plates. Top each with a slice of ham and cover to keep warm.

Meanwhile, fill a large skillet with water and bring to a boil over high heat. Reduce the heat to medium high and add a pinch of salt. Break the eggs into the simmering water and poach until the whites are firm and set, about 5 minutes. Using a slotted spoon, transfer the eggs onto the toasts. Season with salt and pepper. Cover with Hollandaise sauce and serve at once.

Hollandaise Sauce

MAKES ¾ CUP

½ cup (1 stick) unsalted butter
2 large egg yolks
2 tablespoons cold water

1 tablespoon lemon juice
¼ teaspoon salt
Cayenne pepper

In a small heavy saucepan over medium-low heat, melt the butter. Remove from the heat and let stand for 2 minutes so that the whey will separate from the butter. Pour off and reserve the clear butter. Discard the whey.

Combine the egg yolks and cold water in a nonreactive bowl that will fit over a pan of hot water without letting the water touch the bottom of the bowl. Whisk the egg yolks until creamy and slightly thickened. Gradually add the butter, whisking constantly, until all of the butter has been added and the sauce is thickened, 5 minutes. Remove from the heat and stir in the lemon juice. Season with salt and a pinch of cayenne pepper.

Egg and Onion Pie

MAKES ONE 10-INCH PIE (24 APPETIZER SERVINGS)

1 recipe Pie Pastry (recipe follows)
2 tablespoons (¼ stick) unsalted butter
2 large onions, thinly sliced
2 large eggs
2 large egg yolks
1 cup milk

½ cup heavy cream
1 tablespoon snipped chives
1 tablespoon chopped fresh parsley
Salt and freshly ground black pepper to
   taste

Roll out the pastry into a ⅛-inch-thick circle 11 inches in diameter. Line a 10-inch quiche dish or pie plate with the pastry and prick all over with a fork. Decoratively crimp the edges. Chill for 20 minutes, or until firm.

Preheat the oven to 400°F. Tear off a large piece of aluminum foil and place it on top of the pastry, covering the sides. Fill with dried beans, dry rice, or aluminum pie weights to prevent the dough from puffing as it cooks. Cook for about 10 minutes, or until the pastry is lightly browned. Remove from the oven, lift out the weights, and cool. Reduce the oven temperature to 350°F.

In a large heavy skillet over medium-high heat, melt the butter. Add the onions, reduce the heat to low, and cook, stirring often, until the onions are very soft but not brown, about 20 minutes. Transfer to a small bowl and cool.

In a small bowl, beat the eggs, egg yolks, milk, cream, chives, parsley, and salt and pepper. Spread the cooled onions over the bottom of the pastry and pour over the egg mixture. Bake for about 30 minutes, or until the filling is browned and just set. Cool for 10 minutes before cutting into wedges.

Pie Pastry

2 cups flour
1 teaspoon salt
2 tablespoons sugar (for sweet pastry)
⅓ cup unsalted butter, cut into small
  pieces and chilled

⅓ cup chilled vegetable shortening or
  lard
⅓ cup ice water, or more as needed

Into a large bowl, sift the flour with the salt and sugar, if using. Add the butter and shortening and cut into small pieces with 2 knives or a pastry cutter. (Alternatively, in the bowl of a food processor, combine the flour, salt, and sugar and pulse once or twice to blend. Add the butter and shortening and process until the mixture resembles the texture of coarse meal, about 10 seconds. Transfer to a large bowl.)

Make a well in the center of the mixture and add the water. Mix quickly with a fork to form a soft dough. Add another 1–2 tablespoons cold water if the dough appears to be too dry. Turn out onto a floured work surface and work gently into a rough ball. Wrap in plastic and refrigerate for at least 30 minutes. (The pastry dough can be made up to a day in advance.)

Eggs, Cheese, Vegetarian Dishes, and Savory Pies

Welsh Rarebit with Beer

SERVES 4

This old tavern favorite, sometimes called "Welsh rabbit," has warmed the hearts and souls of weary travelers for years. Although the origin of the word "rarebit" is unknown, all recipes from the eighteenth century until now call for Cheddar cheese, thus affirming its British origins.

1 tablespoon unsalted butter
1 pound grated sharp Cheddar cheese
  (about 4 cups)
¾ cup beer, divided
Dash Tabasco sauce or pinch cayenne
  pepper
1 teaspoon dry mustard

½ teaspoon salt
½ teaspoon Worcestershire sauce
1 large egg, lightly beaten
1 teaspoon cornstarch
Toast or broiled tomato halves, for
  serving

In the top of a double boiler set over hot, not boiling, water, melt the butter. Stir in the cheese and all but 1 tablespoon of the beer. Stir until the cheese melts. Add the remaining tablespoon of beer, the Tabasco sauce or cayenne pepper, mustard, salt, and Worcestershire sauce.

In a small bowl, beat the egg with the cornstarch. Stir into the cheese mixture and cook, stirring often, until thickened, about 3–5 minutes. Serve immediately over toast or broiled tomato halves.

WHY DOESN'T WELSH RABBIT CONTAIN RABBIT? INSTEAD, THIS DISH, WHICH IS CALLED A "SAVOURY" IN ENGLAND, CONSISTS OF A PIECE OF TOAST COVERED WITH MELTED CHEESE TO WHICH SEASONINGS AND BEER HAVE BEEN ADDED. ALMOST CERTAINLY, "RABBIT" COMES FROM "RAREBIT," SINCE WELSH RABBIT IS A RARE BIT INDEED.

Shirred Eggs with Surry Sausage

SERVES 2

Surry is a small village across the James River from Williamsburg. Known for the production of delicious country hams, Surry also produces fine sausages. Any smoked link sausage can be substituted with only a slight loss of authenticity.

2 tablespoons vegetable oil
4 links smoked sausage (4 ounces each),
   preferably from Surry
1 small onion, finely chopped
½ green bell pepper, finely chopped

1 large tomato, peeled, seeded, and
   chopped
4 large eggs
Salt and freshly ground black pepper to
   taste

Preheat the oven to 375°F. and butter 2 individual baking dishes that measure 5 inches in diameter. (Enameled cast-iron dishes work best but any glass or porcelain dish will do.)

In a small skillet over medium-high heat, heat the oil. Add the sausages and cook, turning often, until browned on all sides, about 5 minutes. Drain on paper towels. Pour off all but 1 tablespoon of fat from the skillet.

Return the skillet to the heat and add the onion and green pepper. Cook, stirring often, until softened, about 3 minutes. Add the tomato and cook until almost all of the moisture has evaporated, 3–5 minutes. Divide this mixture between the 2 baking dishes. Place 2 sausage links in each dish, allowing room for the eggs.

Make a hollow in the tomato mixture in each dish. Drop 2 eggs into each hollow, being careful not to break the yolks. Season with salt and pepper. Bake for about 10 minutes, uncovered, or until the egg white is set but the yolk is still soft. Serve at once.

Open-Faced Omelette

SERVES 2

1 medium firm-fleshed potato,
    preferably Yukon Gold, peeled and cut
    into ½-inch dice
Salt to taste
4 strips bacon (about 4 ounces), coarsely
    chopped
1 medium onion, finely chopped

1 celery rib, finely chopped
1 medium tomato, peeled, seeded, and
    chopped
Freshly ground black pepper to taste
1 teaspoon chopped fresh thyme
6 large eggs

In a small saucepan, place the potato and add enough cold water to cover. Add salt and bring to a boil over medium-high heat. Reduce the heat to medium and cook until tender but firm, about 10 minutes. Drain.

In an 8-inch ovenproof skillet, place the bacon. Cook over medium heat, stirring often, until the bacon is lightly browned and crisp, about 5 minutes. Using a slotted spoon, remove the bacon and drain on paper towels. Pour off all but 1 tablespoon of the fat. Add the onion and celery to the skillet. Cook over medium-high heat, stirring often, until softened, about 3 minutes. Stir in the tomato and cook until most of the liquid that the tomato gives off has evaporated and the mixture has thickened, 5–7 minutes. Season with salt and pepper. Stir in the thyme.

Preheat the oven to 375°F.

Add the potato to the tomato mixture in the skillet. Stir in the cooked bacon. In a small bowl, beat the eggs with salt and pepper. Pour the eggs into the skillet and gently stir to combine. Cook over medium-high heat for 2–3 minutes to set the bottom of the omelette. Place the skillet in the oven and cook, uncovered, until firm in the center and lightly browned on top, about 12 minutes.

To serve, run a knife around the edge of the skillet to loosen the omelette. Using a spatula, gently lift from underneath and tilt the pan so that the omelette slides in one whole piece onto a cutting surface. Cut into wedges and serve at once.

Gloucester Cheddar Cheese Soufflé

SERVES 4–6

Imported English Cheddar gives this soufflé a distinctively sharp flavor.
A soufflé waits for no one, so have guests seated and ready to eat before serving.

FOR THE BASE
½ cup (1 stick) unsalted butter
½ cup flour
2 cups milk
½ teaspoon salt
Dash Tabasco sauce or pinch cayenne
  pepper

2 cups grated good-quality Cheddar
  cheese, preferably Gloucester
6 large egg yolks
1½ teaspoons dry mustard

TO FINISH THE SOUFFLÉ
6 large egg whites at room temperature

In a large saucepan over medium heat, melt the butter. Add the flour and stir until well blended and lemon colored, about 3 minutes. Pour in the milk, increase the heat to high, and bring to a boil, stirring often. Reduce the heat to medium and simmer until thick and smooth, about 10 minutes. Stir in the salt and Tabasco sauce or cayenne pepper. Remove from the heat. Stir in the cheese. Add the egg yolks, one at a time, and beat well after each addition. Beat in the mustard and set the mixture aside to cool.

To finish the soufflé, preheat the oven to 375°F. and butter a 2-quart soufflé dish. Beat the egg whites until they hold stiff peaks. Gently fold the cooled cheese mixture into the whites and pour into the prepared dish. Bake for 15 minutes, then reduce the temperature to 300°F. Bake for 30–40 minutes longer, or until puffed, golden brown on top, and set in the center. Serve at once.

Bubble and Squeak

SERVES 8

*A vegetarian adaptation of an old English favorite, Bubble and Squeak
derives its name from the sounds it makes while cooking.*

4–5 large all-purpose potatoes
  (4 pounds), peeled and quartered
Salt
¼ cup olive oil, divided
1 medium head green cabbage
  (2 pounds), halved, cored, and thinly
  shredded

Freshly ground black pepper to taste
1 large egg, lightly beaten
1 tablespoon finely snipped chives
  or 2 scallions, trimmed and thinly
  sliced

In a large saucepan, place the potatoes and pour in enough cold water to cover. Add salt to taste and bring to a boil over high heat. Reduce the heat to medium high and cook until the potatoes are very tender, 20–25 minutes. Drain well and puree in a food mill or potato ricer or pass through a fine-mesh sieve. Transfer to a large bowl.

In a large skillet, heat half the oil. Add the cabbage and season with salt and pepper. Cook over medium-high heat, stirring often, until the cabbage is tender and most of the moisture has evaporated, about 10 minutes. Cool slightly in the skillet.

Add the cabbage, egg, chives or scallions, and salt and pepper to the potatoes. Mix well to blend and divide into 16 equal portions. Use your dampened hands to form thick patties.

In a large skillet over medium-high heat, heat the remaining oil. Add the patties and cook, turning once or twice, until golden brown on both sides, 7–10 minutes. Drain on paper towels and season with salt and pepper before serving.

Shields Tavern Grilled Polenta with Garden Vegetables

SERVES 6

Vary the vegetables according to what is in season. Eggplant, mushrooms, carrots, spring onions, fresh beans, or peas can be added or substituted as desired.

2 cups coarse polenta flour
Salt
2 tablespoons olive oil, plus more for brushing
1 onion, thinly sliced
1 green or red bell pepper, cored and thinly sliced
1 clove garlic, minced

1 small zucchini, thinly sliced
1 yellow squash, thinly sliced
2 medium tomatoes, peeled, seeded, and chopped
Freshly ground black pepper to taste
1 recipe Herbed Tomato Sauce (recipe follows)

Place the polenta in a large measuring cup to facilitate pouring. In a large saucepan over high heat, bring 6 cups water to a boil and add 1 teaspoon salt. Reduce the heat to medium high and slowly add the polenta, whisking constantly. Pour in a steady slow stream and do not stop whisking. The mixture will thicken and start to bubble. Reduce the heat to low and cook, stirring frequently, until the mixture is very thick and pulls away from the side of the pan, 30–40 minutes. Transfer to a large flat baking tray and spread out to form a rectangle that measures about ¾-inch thick. Cool completely.

In a large skillet over medium-high heat, heat the olive oil. Add the onion and pepper. Cook, stirring often, until softened, about 5 minutes. Stir in the garlic and cook 1 minute longer. Add the zucchini, yellow squash, and tomatoes. Lower the heat to medium and cook, stirring often, until the tomatoes start to give off their liquid and the squash is translucent, about 10 minutes. Season with salt and pepper.

Preheat a grill or broiler. Cut the cooled polenta into wedges or slices and brush on both sides with olive oil. Grill over high heat or broil until crisp and brown, about 3 minutes per side.

Reheat the vegetable mixture if necessary. Place the grilled polenta in the center of warmed plates and spoon over the vegetables. Serve with the herbed tomato sauce.

Herbed Tomato Sauce

MAKES 2 CUPS

2 tablespoons (¼ stick) unsalted
   butter
1 onion, finely chopped
3–4 ripe tomatoes (1 pound), peeled,
   seeded, and chopped, or 1 (28-ounce)
   can tomatoes, drained and chopped

1 tablespoon chopped fresh basil or
   1 teaspoon dried basil
1½ teaspoons chopped fresh oregano or
   1 teaspoon dried oregano
Salt and freshly ground black pepper to
   taste

In a large saucepan over medium-high heat, melt the butter. Add the onion and cook, stirring often, until softened, 3–5 minutes. Stir in the tomatoes and reduce the heat to medium low. Add the basil, oregano, and salt and pepper. Simmer, partially covered, stirring often, until the tomatoes are pulpy and the sauce is thickened, about 15 minutes.

Transfer the sauce to a food processor or blender and puree until smooth. Season again with salt and pepper before using.

Eggs, Cheese, Vegetarian Dishes, and Savory Pies

Macaroni and Cheese

SERVES 4

*Homemade macaroni and cheese is a main-dish vegetarian delight. Nourishing and
satisfying, this classic can also be served as a side dish with meat and poultry.
Use a good-quality imported Cheddar for best results.*

Salt
½ pound dried macaroni
4 tablespoons (½ stick) unsalted butter,
  divided
2 tablespoons flour
1 cup milk

2 cups (loosely packed) grated sharp
  Cheddar cheese
Freshly ground black pepper to taste
1 cup fresh bread crumbs
2 tablespoons grated Parmesan cheese

Fill a large saucepan with water, add salt, and bring to a boil over high heat. Add the
macaroni, bring back to a boil, and cook for 5 minutes. Drain and rinse under cold
running water. Drain again and transfer to a large bowl.

In a medium saucepan over medium-high heat, melt half the butter. Whisk in the
flour and cook, stirring often, until smooth and lemon colored, about 3 minutes. Pour
in the milk, increase the heat to high, and bring to a boil. Reduce the heat to medium
and cook, uncovered, stirring often, until the sauce is slightly reduced and thick
enough to coat the back of a spoon, about 10 minutes. Remove from the heat and stir
in the Cheddar cheese until melted. Season with salt and pepper.

Preheat the oven to 375°F. and butter a 2-quart baking dish. Pour the sauce over
the macaroni and stir well. Pour into the baking dish. In a small bowl, mix together the
bread crumbs and Parmesan cheese and sprinkle the mixture over the top of the dish.
Melt the remaining half of the butter and drizzle over the bread crumb mixture. Bake
until the top is browned and the sauce is bubbling, 20–25 minutes. Serve hot.

Christiana Campbell's Tavern Vermicelli Pies

SERVES 6

2 recipes Pie Pastry (page 63)
½ pound dried vermicelli pasta
2 tablespoons (¼ stick) unsalted butter
1¼ pounds mushrooms, trimmed and
  sliced
½ pound shiitake mushrooms, trimmed
  and sliced
2 small shallots, minced
1½ pounds fresh spinach, washed,
  trimmed of large stems, and chopped

3–4 scallions, trimmed and thinly sliced
½ cup dry white wine
1 cup heavy cream
2 cups grated sharp Cheddar cheese
  (about ½ pound)
2 large eggs, lightly beaten
1 teaspoon salt
¼ teaspoon grated nutmeg
1 recipe Herbed Tomato Sauce
  (page 71)

Butter six 2-cup soufflé molds. Roll out the pastry to a thickness of about ⅛ inch. Using one of the molds as a template, cut out 6 circles that will just fit inside the perimeter of the mold and form top crusts when baked. Layer the circles between sheets of waxed paper and refrigerate until ready to bake.

Bring a large pot of salted water to a boil over high heat. Add the pasta and bring back to a boil. Cook, stirring often, until almost tender, about 10 minutes. Drain in a large colander and rinse under cold running water.

Preheat the oven to 375°F. In a large saucepan over medium-high heat, melt the butter. Add all the mushrooms, the shallots, spinach, and scallions. Cook, stirring often, until the spinach has completely wilted and the shallots are tender, about 5 minutes. Pour in the wine and increase the heat to high. Boil until the alcohol has evaporated, about 2 minutes. Pour in the cream and cook until the mixture is slightly thickened, about 4 minutes. Transfer to a large bowl and cool. Stir in the vermicelli, cheese, eggs, salt, and nutmeg. Blend well and divide the mixture among the 6 molds. Top each mold with a circle of pastry. Bake until the crusts are lightly browned, 25–30 minutes. Run a knife around the perimeter of each pie and invert onto individual serving plates. Serve with herbed tomato sauce.

King's Arms Tavern Spinach Pie

SERVES 6

2 recipes Pie Pastry (page 63)
2 pounds cooked or thawed frozen
   spinach, squeezed dry
2 tablespoons (¼ stick) unsalted butter
1 large onion, finely chopped
1 cup tightly packed grated Swiss cheese
3 large eggs

1 cup milk
½ cup heavy cream
¼ teaspoon salt
⅛ teaspoon freshly grated black pepper
⅛ teaspoon grated nutmeg
1 large egg yolk, beaten
1 tablespoon heavy cream

Roll out half the pastry to a circle with a thickness of ⅛ inch. Line a 9-inch pie pan with the pastry. Prick all over with a fork, cover with plastic wrap, and refrigerate for at least 30 minutes. For the top crust, roll out the other half of the pastry into a ⅛-inch-thick circle slightly larger than the pie pan. Place flat on a baking sheet, cover with plastic wrap, and refrigerate until the pie is assembled. (The pie pan can be lined and the top crust rolled out flat up to 2 days ahead if kept tightly covered in the refrigerator.)

Preheat the oven to 425°F. Fill the lined pie pan with parchment paper or foil. Add

pie weights, dried beans, or rice to keep the pastry from puffing while cooking. Cook the pastry until lightly browned around the edges, about 10 minutes. Carefully lift off the paper or foil and the weights. Reduce the oven temperature to 375°F. and return the pan to the oven. Bake until the center of the pastry is white and dry, about 5 minutes longer. Cool.

Coarsely chop the spinach. In a medium saucepan over medium-high heat, melt the butter. Add the onion and cook, stirring often, until softened, 3–5 minutes. Stir in the chopped spinach.

Preheat the oven to 375°F. Sprinkle half the cheese in the bottom of the cooled pastry shell. Top with half the spinach and onion mixture. Add another layer of cheese and the remaining spinach and onion. In a small bowl, beat the eggs with the milk, cream, salt, pepper, and nutmeg. Ladle in just enough of this custard mixture to barely cover the pie filling.

Lay the rolled-out circle of pastry over the filled pie pan. Trim the edges with scissors and crimp decoratively to seal. In a small bowl, mix the egg yolk with the cream to make an egg glaze. Brush with the egg glaze and cut a small hole in the center of the top crust for the steam to escape. Place the pie on a baking sheet and bake until the crust is golden brown and the filling is bubbling, 40–45 minutes. Let the pie rest at room temperature for 10 minutes before slicing.

Eggs, Cheese, Vegetarian Dishes, and Savory Pies

Pot Likker Greens with Dumplings

SERVES 4

*Pot likker is the broth that comes from cooking greens. Mustard greens,
collard greens, turnip greens, and kale have been a part of traditional southern
cooking for years. This one-dish meal calls for dumplings, an unusual
and delicious way to absorb the flavorful broth.*

FOR THE POT LIKKER
2 cups Vegetable Stock (recipe follows)
   or low-salt canned vegetable stock
1 pound greens (mustard, collard, kale,
   or turnip greens), trimmed and
   thoroughly cleaned
1 large onion, quartered
1 medium carrot, peeled and coarsely
   chopped
1 celery rib, coarsely chopped
3 heads fresh garlic, halved horizontally
Salt
1 teaspoon whole peppercorns
Several sprigs fresh parsley

1 bay leaf, crumbled
1 medium white turnip, peeled and cut
   into ½-inch cubes
1 medium white potato, peeled and cut
   into ½-inch cubes
Freshly ground black pepper to taste

FOR THE DUMPLINGS
2 cups flour
1 teaspoon salt
1 tablespoon baking powder
1 tablespoon vegetable shortening
¾ cup milk

In a large soup pot or kettle over high heat, place the stock and bring to a boil. Cut the greens into wide strips and add to the pot. Add the onion, carrot, celery, garlic, 1 teaspoon salt, peppercorns, parsley, and bay leaf. Add enough water to cover the vegetables, if needed. Reduce the heat to medium and simmer, partially covered, until the vegetables are very tender and the broth has a rich, full flavor, about 45 minutes.

Use a slotted spoon to remove the cooked greens to a bowl and cool. Strain the remaining contents of the pot, discarding all solids. Return the strained liquid to the pot and add the turnip and potato. Cook over medium heat until tender, about 10 minutes. Coarsely chop the greens and add to the pot. Season with salt and pepper. Bring to a simmer over medium-high heat.

To make the dumplings, into a large bowl, sift the flour, salt, and baking powder. Blend in the shortening with a pastry blender or fork. Add the milk and mix well.

Dip a teaspoon into cold water and then into the dough. Spoon the dumplings on top of the pot likker. Cover and cook for 15 minutes without lifting the lid. Ladle into warmed bowls and serve hot.

Vegetable Stock

MAKES 2 QUARTS

3 onions, quartered
3 carrots, thickly sliced
2 celery ribs, thickly sliced
3 leeks, white part only, thickly sliced
2 turnips, quartered
1 bay leaf

Several sprigs thyme
1 teaspoon whole black peppercorns
1 teaspoon salt
2 pounds all-purpose potatoes, peeled
  and cut into ¾-inch pieces

In a large soup pot or kettle, combine the onions, carrots, celery, leeks, turnips, bay leaf, thyme, peppercorns, and salt. Pour in enough cold water to cover. Bring to a boil over medium-high heat, reduce the heat to medium low, and cook, partially covered, for 2 hours. Add the potatoes during the last hour of cooking time. Strain, cool to room temperature, and refrigerate until ready to use.

Fish

and

Shellfish

Good Eating

AN astonishing array of fresh and saltwater seafood comes from the Atlantic Ocean, Chesapeake Bay, and the rivers, tributaries, and creeks of Tidewater Virginia. During the seventeenth and eighteenth centuries, it was said that much of the James and York Rivers were so full of oyster banks that ship captains were forced to steer around them.

"As for Fish, both of Fresh and Salt-Water, of Shell-Fish, and others," wrote historian Robert Beverley, "no Country can boast of more Variety, greater Plenty, or of better in their several Kinds." Gentlemen anglers like Beverley may have baited a hook in their leisure, but many other Virginians, including slaves, fished and crabbed to supplement their diet or worked as watermen.

Delicious seafood dishes have graced Tidewater Virginia tables for generations. Williamsburg taverns afford diners many opportunities to enjoy modern adaptations of these fish and shellfish dishes. The recipes in this section include regional specialties, old-time favorites, and a few recent additions.

PREVIOUS PAGES: Collops of Salmon with Braised Winter Cabbage and Fennel Seeds.

Collops of Salmon with
Braised Winter Cabbage and Fennel Seeds

12 thin slices salmon (3 ounces each)
3 tablespoons unsalted butter
2 tablespoons fennel seeds
1 small head cabbage, tough core
   removed and thinly shredded
2 tablespoons red wine vinegar

Salt and freshly ground black pepper to
   taste
1 cup flour
3 tablespoons vegetable oil
Lemon wedges and chopped parsley, for
   garnish

Working with one slice at a time, place the salmon between 2 pieces of plastic wrap. Use a heavy rolling pin, the back of a knife, or a mallet to pound each ½-inch thick. Place the slices on a plate and refrigerate, tightly covered, until ready to serve.

In a large skillet over medium heat, melt the butter. Add the fennel seeds and cook, stirring often, until lightly browned, about 2 minutes. Stir in the cabbage and vinegar, season with salt and pepper, and reduce the heat to low. Cover and cook, stirring often, until the cabbage is very tender, about 45 minutes. Check often. Add small amounts of water if necessary to prevent scorching.

Season the pounded salmon slices on both sides with salt and pepper. In a large shallow bowl, place the flour and add the salmon, one slice at a time. Turn to coat and shake off the excess flour. In a large skillet over high heat, heat the vegetable oil. Add the salmon and cook until golden brown, about 2 minutes on each side.

Place the cabbage on a warmed serving platter and arrange the salmon slices on top, overlapping. Garnish with the lemon wedges and parsley.

Christiana Campbell's Tavern Crab Cakes

SERVES 4

Sally Lunn (page 163) or egg bread can be used to make the bread crumbs
that bind the cakes together. Form the cakes gently.
Too much handling will render them compact and tough.

1 pound lump or backfin crabmeat
3 slices white sandwich bread, crusts
  removed
½ cup mayonnaise
1 tablespoon Dijon mustard
3 tablespoons chopped fresh parsley
2 scallions, finely chopped

1 large egg, lightly beaten
1 tablespoon Worcestershire sauce
1 tablespoon lemon juice
Salt and freshly ground black pepper to
  taste
2 tablespoons (¼ stick) unsalted butter
2 tablespoons vegetable oil

Pick over the crabmeat to remove all cartilage and shell. Place the bread in a food processor and process for about 30 seconds to make fine, soft bread crumbs.

In a large bowl, combine the mayonnaise, mustard, parsley, scallions, egg, Worcestershire sauce, and lemon juice. Add the crab and bread crumbs. Gently stir just to mix and season with salt and pepper.

Divide the mixture into 8 uniform balls. Use your hands to form them into small, round cakes. Transfer to a plate or platter, cover, and chill for 30 minutes.

In a large skillet over medium-high heat, melt the butter with the oil. Add the crab cakes and cook until golden brown, about 3 minutes on each side. Drain on paper towels and serve at once.

Soft-Shell Crabs with Capers and Lemon Butter

SERVES 4

You can buy soft-shell crabs already cleaned; just ask your fishmonger to do this for you.

12 soft-shell crabs, cleaned
1 cup flour
1 teaspoon salt
½ cup (1 stick) unsalted butter, melted, plus 2 tablespoons (¼ stick) unsalted butter

2 tablespoons vegetable oil
¼ cup finely chopped fresh parsley
2 tablespoons capers, drained and finely chopped
2 tablespoons lemon juice

Pat the crabs dry with paper towels. Mix the flour and salt in a shallow bowl. Dip the crabs into the flour, one at a time, and shake off any excess flour.

In a large skillet over medium-high heat, melt the 2 tablespoons butter with the oil. Add enough of the crabs to fit in the skillet snugly without overcrowding. (Cook the crabs in batches if necessary. If the skillet is too full, the crabs will not brown properly.) Cook, turning often, until lightly browned and crisp, 2–3 minutes per side. Drain on paper towels. Sprinkle with more salt if desired.

In a small saucepan, melt the ½ cup butter with the parsley, capers, and lemon juice over low heat. Arrange the crabs on a large platter and drizzle with a small amount of the butter. Spoon the capers over. Serve warm with the remaining butter on the side.

King's Arms Tavern Flounder
Stuffed with Crabmeat and Shrimp

SERVES 6

FOR THE STUFFING
¼ cup (½ stick) unsalted butter
1 small onion, finely chopped
1 celery rib, finely chopped
¼ pound medium shrimp, cooked and
　diced
½ pound lump or backfin crabmeat
1 tablespoon finely chopped fresh
　parsley
½ teaspoon paprika
Salt and freshly ground black pepper to
　taste

¼ cup dry white wine
1½ cups fresh bread crumbs

FOR THE FISH
6 flounder fillets (6 ounces each)
3 tablespoons lemon juice
Salt and freshly ground black pepper to
　taste
1 cup fresh bread crumbs
½ cup (1 stick) unsalted butter, melted

To make the stuffing, in a large saucepan over medium-high heat, melt the butter. Add the onion and celery. Cook, stirring often, until softened, 3–5 minutes. Stir in the shrimp, crabmeat, and parsley. Season with paprika and salt and pepper. Add the wine and reduce the heat to medium. Cook, stirring often, until the mixture is warmed through, about 5 minutes. Remove from the heat and stir in the bread crumbs.

To bake the fish, preheat the oven to 375°F. and butter a 2-quart baking dish.

Spread each fillet with 2–3 tablespoons of the stuffing. Roll and fasten with tooth-picks. Place in the baking dish and season with the lemon juice and salt and pepper. Sprinkle over the bread crumbs and drizzle with the melted butter.

Bake until the fish flakes easily when tested with a fork, about 20 minutes.

Oyster and Lobster Pies

SERVES 8

Recipes for oyster and lobster pies were included in several eighteenth-century cookbooks. These individual pies are good for entertaining. The casseroles or ramekins can be filled ahead and refrigerated for up to two days or frozen for a week or two. Top with the pastry rounds and brush with the egg wash just before baking.

10 tablespoons (1¼ sticks) unsalted butter, divided
6 tablespoons flour
1¾ cups Fish Stock (page 96) or bottled clam juice
¼ cup dry white wine
12 ounces lobster meat, diced
½ pound mushrooms, thinly sliced

1 pint oysters, drained
2 teaspoons lemon juice
½ cup dry sherry
Salt and freshly ground black pepper to taste
1 recipe Pie Pastry (page 63)
1 large egg yolk mixed with 1 teaspoon water

Preheat the oven to 400°F. 10 minutes before baking the pies. Butter 8 individual casseroles or ramekins.

In a large saucepan over medium heat, melt 4 tablespoons of the butter. Add the flour and stir until well blended and lemon colored, about 3 minutes. Pour in the fish stock, increase the heat to high, and bring to a boil. Reduce the heat to medium and whisk until the mixture is smooth and thick. Add the white wine and simmer, partially covered, stirring often, until reduced and thickened, 15–20 minutes.

In a large skillet over medium heat, melt 2 tablespoons of the butter. Add the lobster meat and cook, stirring often, for 2 minutes. Add the lobster to the mixture.

In the skillet, melt the remaining 4 tablespoons of the butter. Add the mushrooms and cook, stirring often, until most

NOT SO LONG AGO, EXTENSIVE OYSTER BEDS THREATENED TO INTERFERE WITH NAVIGATION IN HAMPTON ROADS. ALTHOUGH THE CROP IS MUCH REDUCED NOW, THE LUSCIOUS BIVALVE REMAINS A VIRGINIA FAVORITE.

of the liquid has cooked away, about 5 minutes. Add the mushrooms. Stir in the oysters, lemon juice, sherry, and salt and pepper. Pour the mixture into the casseroles.

Working with one quarter of the pastry at a time, roll out the dough ⅛-inch thick. To top each casserole, cut out circles of pastry large enough to seal the edges to the rim. Use the tip of a very sharp paring knife to cut a small hole in the center to allow the steam to escape. Prick the pastry with a fork and brush with the egg yolk and water mixture. Bake for 30 minutes, or until golden brown. Serve hot.

Christiana Campbell's Tavern Oyster Fritters
with Dipping Sauce

SERVES 4

*Since 1607, when Captains John Smith and Christopher Newport landed in
Jamestown and found an abundance of oysters "lying thick as stones,"
oysters have been a staple of the Virginian diet. The oysters are left whole
in the batter to keep their juicy shape and creamy texture.
The dipping sauce that accompanies this dish is reminiscent of creamy cocktail
sauce made with tomato ketchup mixed with mayonnaise and horseradish.
An early recipe for tomato ketchup appeared in* The Virginia Housewife *in 1824.*

FOR THE DIPPING SAUCE
¾ cup ketchup
2 tablespoons drained bottled
   horseradish or more to taste
¾ cup mayonnaise

FOR THE OYSTER FRITTERS
6 tablespoons flour, plus more for
   dredging
⅔ cup lukewarm water

2 tablespoons vegetable oil
1 tablespoon finely chopped fresh
   parsley
2 large egg whites, stiffly beaten
Vegetable oil for frying
24 shucked medium oysters, drained
Salt and freshly ground black pepper
   to taste
Lemon wedges, for garnish

To prepare the sauce, in a small bowl, combine the ketchup, horseradish, and mayonnaise and stir well. Chill until ready to serve.

To make the fritter batter, in a large bowl, combine the flour, water, oil, and parsley. Whisk until smooth. Stir about one quarter of the egg whites into the mixture to lighten. Gently fold in the rest.

Fill an electric deep-fat fryer or large skillet with enough oil to measure 1–1½ inches deep. Heat to 375°F. Dip the oysters in the additional flour and drop into the batter. Transfer the batter-dipped oysters to the hot fat and fry, turning, until golden brown, 1–2 minutes. Sprinkle with salt and pepper. Drain well on paper towels and serve warm with the dipping sauce. Garnish with the lemon wedges.

*OPPOSITE: King's Arms Tavern Fried Oyster Sandwiches ("Po' Boys") with Tarragon Mayonnaise,
top, and Christiana Campbell's Tavern Oyster Fritters with Dipping Sauce, bottom.*

King's Arms Tavern Fried Oyster Sandwiches ("Po' Boys") with Tarragon Mayonnaise

SERVES 4

The English served oysters in hollowed-out bread as far back as the seventeenth century, and Mary Randolph mentioned an "oyster loaf" in The Virginia Housewife *(1824). The southern "Po' Boy," as this sandwich is called today, is messy to eat but delightfully delicious.*

FOR THE TARRAGON MAYONNAISE
2 tablespoons chopped fresh tarragon
¼ cup red wine vinegar
1 large shallot, minced
1 cup mayonnaise
Salt and freshly ground black pepper to taste

FOR THE FRIED OYSTERS
Vegetable oil for frying
24 shucked oysters, drained

2 cups flour
½ teaspoon salt
¼ teaspoon freshly ground black pepper
2 large eggs
1 cup milk
2 cups cracker crumbs

FOR THE SANDWICHES
1 loaf French or Italian bread
Several large lettuce leaves, washed and trimmed

To make the mayonnaise, in a small heavy saucepan, combine the tarragon, vinegar, and shallot. Bring to a boil over high heat, stirring often. Reduce the heat to medium and cook until almost all of the liquid has evaporated and the shallots are very soft. (The time will vary according to the size of the pan. Watch carefully, as the shallots will burn quickly and make the mayonnaise bitter.) Cool to room temperature, then stir into the mayonnaise. Season with salt and pepper. Chill well before serving.

To fry the oysters, into a large skillet, pour enough vegetable oil to measure a depth of 1 inch. Heat over medium-high heat until hot but not smoking. (Alternatively, fill an electric deep-fat fryer with vegetable oil and set the temperature at 375°F.) Pick over the oysters to remove any bits of shell.

In a large bowl, mix together the flour, salt, and pepper. In a small bowl, beat the eggs with the milk. In another bowl, place the cracker crumbs. Coat each oyster with flour, dip in the egg mixture, and roll in the cracker crumbs. Fry in the hot oil, turning often, until golden brown, about 5 minutes. Drain on paper towels.

Cut the bread in half lengthwise and scoop out some of the center. Fill the bottom half with the fried oysters and spoon the mayonnaise over. Add the lettuce leaves and cover with the top half of the bread. Cut into 4 pieces and serve at once.

Travis House Oysters

This dish takes its name from Colonel Edward Champion Travis, a member of the House of Burgesses, who built the Travis House in 1765. It was the site of a restaurant run by Colonial Williamsburg from 1930 until 1951. Travis House Oysters was a favorite dish there and remains popular at the King's Arms Tavern today.

2 quarts oysters with their liquor
1 small onion, finely chopped
½ teaspoon Tabasco sauce or more to
  taste

3 cups crushed saltine crackers
Salt and freshly ground black pepper to
  taste
½ cup (1 stick) unsalted butter, melted

Preheat the oven to 400°F. and butter a 2-quart baking dish.

In a large bowl, mix together the oysters, onion, and Tabasco sauce.

Spread 1 cup of the cracker crumbs evenly over the bottom of the baking dish. Add a layer of half the oysters, season with salt and pepper, and drizzle a third of the butter over. Add another layer of cracker crumbs and the remaining half of the oysters. Season with salt and pepper, drizzle another third of the butter over, and sprinkle the remaining crumbs over. Drizzle the remaining butter over the top and bake for 20–30 minutes, or until hot and bubbly.

Seafood Muddle

SERVES 4–6

In this recipe from the Barrier Islands, tomatoes and aromatic vegetables are stewed with seafood. "Muddle" comes from early settlers and means a "mess of fish."

2 tablespoons vegetable oil
2 large onions, thinly sliced
2 medium carrots, peeled and finely chopped
1 celery rib, thinly sliced
1 clove garlic, minced
1 (16-ounce) can tomatoes, drained, seeded, and chopped
2 medium all-purpose potatoes, cut into ½-inch dice
6 cups Fish Stock (page 96) or bottled clam juice

Salt and freshly ground black pepper to taste
Pinch saffron threads (optional)
12 small clams, preferably Little Necks, scrubbed
1 pound lean fish (cod, flounder, bass, or snapper), cut into 2-inch pieces
½ pound medium shrimp, peeled, deveined, and halved
12 small mussels, rinsed and beards removed
¼ cup finely chopped fresh parsley

In a large kettle or soup pot over medium-high heat, heat the oil. Add the onions, carrots, and celery. Cook, stirring often, until softened, 3–5 minutes. Add the garlic and cook 1 minute longer. Stir in the tomatoes and potatoes. Reduce the heat to medium low, cover, and cook until the potatoes are slightly softened, about 10 minutes. Watch carefully and add a few tablespoons of fish stock if necessary to prevent scorching.

Pour in the fish stock and increase the heat to high. Bring to a boil, reduce the heat to medium, and season with salt and pepper. Add the saffron and simmer until the potatoes are completely cooked, 10–15 minutes longer.

Add the clams and cook until they start to open, about 5 minutes. Add the fish, shrimp, and mussels. Cook until the fish is opaque, the shrimp are pink, and the clams and mussels are fully opened, about 10 minutes. (Discard any clams or mussels that remain unopened.) Season with salt and pepper. Sprinkle the parsley over and serve hot in warmed bowls.

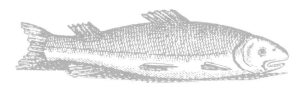

Chowning's Tavern Salmon Cakes

FOR THE CAKES
1 fresh salmon fillet (1 pound), steamed
  or poached, flaked
2 large eggs, lightly beaten
2 tablespoons milk
½ cup fresh bread crumbs
1 small onion, finely chopped
1 celery rib, finely chopped
Salt and freshly ground black pepper to
  taste

FOR COOKING THE CAKES
½ cup flour
½ teaspoon salt
¼ teaspoon freshly ground black pepper
2 large eggs
2 cups fresh bread crumbs
2 tablespoons (¼ stick) unsalted butter
2 tablespoons vegetable oil

FOR SERVING
1 recipe Herbed Tomato Sauce
  (page 71)

In a large bowl, mix together the salmon, eggs, milk, bread crumbs, onion, celery, and salt and pepper. Divide the mixture into 12 small cakes and place on a plate or platter. Cover with plastic wrap and chill for at least 1 hour. (The cakes can be made up to 4 hours in advance.)

To cook the cakes, in a shallow bowl, mix the flour with the salt and pepper. In a separate bowl, beat the eggs with 2 tablespoons water. In a third bowl, place the bread crumbs.

In a large skillet over medium-high heat, melt the butter with the oil. Roll each cake in the seasoned flour to coat thoroughly. Shake off any excess flour and dip in the beaten egg mixture. Drain off any excess egg and transfer to the bread crumbs. Turn the cakes in the crumbs until completely coated.

Cook the cakes in the hot butter and oil mixture until lightly browned, 2–3 minutes on each side. Drain on paper towels and serve at once with the herbed tomato sauce.

Sea Trout Fillets Topped with Crabmeat and Dill Sauce

SERVES 4

Sea trout is actually a southern form of weakfish. It has a sweet, lean flesh and can be quite fragile. Substitute trout, flounder, cod, or sole for the sea trout if desired.

FOR THE DILL SAUCE
1 cup mayonnaise
1 tablespoon finely chopped fresh dill weed
1 teaspoon lemon juice
1 teaspoon Pernod or Ricard (see Note; optional)
Salt and freshly ground white pepper to taste

FOR PREPARING THE FISH
4 sea trout fillets (about 6 ounces each)
Salt and freshly ground black pepper to taste
¼ cup fresh bread crumbs
½ pound lump crabmeat
1 teaspoon grated lemon peel
2 tablespoons (¼ stick) unsalted butter, melted

In a small bowl, mix together the mayonnaise, dill, lemon juice, Pernod or Ricard, and salt and pepper. Cover and refrigerate the sauce until ready to serve.

Preheat the oven to 425°F. and butter a baking dish large enough to hold the fish fillets in one flat layer. Arrange the fish snugly in the dish and season with salt and pepper.

In a small bowl, mix together the bread crumbs, crabmeat, lemon peel, and butter.

Top each fillet with equal amounts of the crabmeat mixture. Bake until the topping is browned and the fish is firm to the touch, 12–15 minutes. Top with a spoonful of the dill sauce and serve the extra sauce on the side. Serve hot.

NOTE: Pernod and Ricard are anise-flavored drinks called *pastis* that are popular in France. Omit if not readily available.

Planked Shad with Shad Roe

SERVES 6

At political rallies and social gatherings throughout Virginia, folks meet to partake of shad planking, a time-honored colonial tradition. The fish is secured on wooden boards and propped up at an angle facing hot coals, while the roe is deep-fried and served on the side. The following do-at-home version calls for fillets, since a whole fish has an intricate pattern of many small bones. Serve on a large platter if suitable planks cannot be found.

FOR THE SHAD ROE
6–8 slices bacon
6 small pairs fresh shad roe
  (8–10 ounces each)
1 cup flour
¾ cup dry white wine
3 tablespoons capers, drained and finely
  chopped
Salt and freshly ground black pepper to
  taste

FOR THE PLANKED SHAD
1 whole boned shad fillet
  (2½–3 pounds), with skin
4 tablespoons (½ stick) unsalted butter,
  melted
Salt and freshly ground black pepper to
  taste

To prepare the roe, in a large skillet over medium-high heat, place the bacon. Cook, turning often, until browned and crisp. Drain on paper towels. Cool and chop finely.

Separate the roe sacs and dry well with paper towels. Dredge the roe in the flour and shake off any excess. Transfer to the skillet and cook over medium-high heat until firm and lightly browned on both sides, about 10 minutes. Remove to a plate or platter and cover with foil to keep warm.

Pour out the fat from the skillet. Add the wine and place over medium-high heat. Cook, whisking constantly, until reduced by half and slightly thickened. Add the capers and season with salt and pepper. Combine with the roe, cover, and keep warm.

Meanwhile, to cook the shad, carefully check that all bones have been removed from the fillet. Preheat the broiler to high and position the oven broiling rack 4–5 inches from the source of heat. Oil a broiling pan and place the fish on top, skin side down. Brush with half the melted butter and season with salt and pepper. Broil until the shad is lightly browned and flakes easily, 6–8 minutes. Baste occasionally with the remaining butter.

Carefully transfer the broiled shad to an oak plank large enough to hold both the fish and the roe sacs. Place the shad in the middle of the plank and surround with the roe. Spoon the white wine and caper reduction over the roe, sprinkle the bacon over, and serve at once.

Fish and Shellfish

Curried Shrimp

*Serve on a large platter with rice and surround with small bowls of
condiments such as shredded coconut, toasted almonds, chutney,
chopped crisp bacon, or sieved hard-cooked eggs.*

¼ cup (½ stick) unsalted butter
1 small onion, thinly sliced
1 celery rib, thinly sliced
2 teaspoons mild curry powder or to
  taste
3 tablespoons flour
2 cups Fish Stock (recipe follows)
½ cup heavy cream

Salt and freshly ground black pepper to
  taste
2 pounds medium shrimp, peeled and
  deveined
¼ cup golden raisins
1 tablespoon finely chopped fresh
  parsley

In a medium saucepan over medium-high heat, melt the butter. Add the onion and celery. Cook, stirring often, until softened, 3–5 minutes. Add the curry powder and cook 1 minute longer. Stir in the flour and cook 2 minutes longer. Pour in the fish stock, increase the heat to high, and bring to a boil, stirring often. Reduce the heat to medium and cook until thickened, about 5 minutes. Pour in the cream, season with salt and pepper, and increase the heat to high. Boil until thick enough to coat the back of a spoon thinly, about 3 minutes.

Reduce the heat to medium and add the shrimp and raisins. Cook until the shrimp are curled and opaque, 5–7 minutes. Stir in the parsley just before serving.

Fish Stock

MAKES 2 QUARTS

2 tablespoons (¼ stick) unsalted butter
2 onions, finely chopped
3 pounds lean white fish bones, heads,
  and tails

1 teaspoon salt
½ teaspoon freshly ground black pepper

In a large soup pot or kettle over medium-high heat, melt the butter. Add the onions and cook, stirring often, until softened, 3–5 minutes. Add the fish bones and cook, stirring, until heated through, about 2 minutes.

Pour in enough cold water to cover the bones. Add the salt and pepper, increase the heat to high, and bring to a boil. Reduce the heat to medium low and simmer, partially covered, for 20 minutes. Strain and cool to room temperature. Cover and refrigerate until ready to use.

Broiled Bluefish with Whole-Grain Mustard Sauce

SERVES 4

Bluefish, an old Virginia favorite, is often caught in local waters.
It has a dark flesh and a high oil content, both of which are complemented
by the assertiveness of mustard. Mackerel is a good substitute.

½ cup dry white wine
½ cup heavy cream
¼ cup whole-grain mustard
Salt and freshly ground black pepper to
    taste

4 fresh bluefish fillets (6–8 ounces each)
2 tablespoons (¼ stick) unsalted butter,
    melted

In a small heavy nonreactive saucepan, place the wine. Bring to a boil over high heat. Boil rapidly until only 2 tablespoons remain. Pour in the cream, bring back to a boil, and boil until the liquid is reduced by half. Remove from the heat and stir in the mustard. Season with salt and pepper, cover, and keep warm.

Preheat the broiler to high and position the oven broiling rack 4–5 inches from the source of heat. Oil a broiling pan and place the fillets on top, skin side down. Brush each fillet with melted butter and season with salt and pepper.

Broil until the fish is opaque and firm to the touch, 8–10 minutes. Remove to warmed plates. Gently reheat the mustard sauce over very low heat. Do not boil. Spoon a small amount of the sauce over each fillet and serve at once.

Poultry

and

Game

At a Court of Hystings held for the City of
Williamsburg on the 9 Day of March 1749/50:

The Rates of Liquors, Diet, etc. as settled
by the Court in March last are continued for one
Year till March Court next.

Viz: £   S   D

For each Diet · · · · · · · · · · · · · · · · · · · —   *   —
Lodging for each Person · · · · · · · · · · · —   —   7½
Stable Room & Fodder for each Horse Night· —   —   7½
Stable Room & Fodder for each Horse 24 Hours · —   —   11¼
Each Gallon of Corn or Oats · · · · · · · · · —   —   6
Wine of Virginia produce per Quart · · · · —   5   —
French Brandy per Quart · · · · · · · · · · —   4   —
Sherry & Canary Wine per Quart · · · · · · —   4   4½
Red & White Lisbon & Claret per Quart · —   3   1½
Madeira Wine per Quart · · · · · · · · · · · —   3   —
Fayall Wine per Quart · · · · · · · · · · · · —   1   3
French Brandy Punch & Flip per Quart · · —   1   3
Rum & Virginia Brandy per Quart · · · · · —   2   —
Rum Punch & Flip per Quart · · · · · · · · —   —   7½
Ditto made with White Sugar · · · · —   —   9
Virginia middling Beer per Quart · · · · · —   —   3·¾
Virginia Cyder per Quart · · · · · · · · · · —   —   3·¾
London & Bristol Beer in Bottles per Quart —   1   3
Welch Ale per Bottle · · · · · · · · · · · · · —   1   3
A Quart of Arrack in Punch · · · · · · · · · —   10   —
English Cyder per Quart Bottle · · · · · · —   1   —
Virginia fine white Apple Cyder per Bottle · —   —   6
Virginia Brewed Ale per Quart · · · · · · —   —   7½

THE amount of poultry and game in early America astounded the first explorers and settlers. Spaniards captured wild turkeys in the sixteenth century and took them to Europe, where their domesticated cousins became a delicacy in England long before the first settlers brought chickens to Jamestown. In 1739, botanist John Clayton wrote about the prodigious numbers of wildfowl in Virginia to a friend in England: "Wild Turkey's very numerous, partridges, wild geese, swans, . . . Teal Duck and Mallard, black Ducks . . . wild Pidgeons in prodigious great flocks, . . . Larks as big as Quails."

By the eighteenth century, whether folks ate domesticated fowl or wild-fowl and how much game they consumed depended on their status and where they lived. Archaeological evidence shows that slaves and poor whites, who hunted and trapped in their spare time, ate more wildfowl and game—especially possum, squirrel, and raccoons—than their betters. The middling sort and the gentry raised their own chickens, turkeys, and ducks or bought poultry at the town market. Settlers living on the frontier, where quail, wild turkeys, ducks, deer, rabbits, squirrels, and other small animals were plentiful, favored wildfowl and game.

By 1779, planter James Mercer observed that the "Negroes . . . are the general Chicken merchants" in the Chesapeake. They raised and sold some chickens and eggs and used the rest to round out their diets. Plantation mistresses and Williamsburg housewives often bought chickens and eggs from these slave "merchants," fattening the chickens for a few days before having them killed, plucked, and readied for the spit or cooking pot.

꒦꒷

PREVIOUS PAGES: East India Company Fried Chicken with Christiana Campbell's Tavern Slaw.

Shields Tavern Chicken and Dumplings

SERVES 6

*When properly prepared, no dish evokes the comfort of good home cooking more
than the following all-time favorite. A tender puff of light biscuit set atop
a savory stew brings nostalgic tears to the eyes of many southerners.*

FOR THE CHICKEN
1 stewing chicken (4 to 5 pounds)
1 small onion, sliced
1 carrot, sliced
2 celery ribs, finely chopped
1 teaspoon salt

FOR THE SAUCE
$\frac{1}{4}$ cup ($\frac{1}{2}$ stick) unsalted butter or 4
  tablespoons chicken fat
6 tablespoons flour

$\frac{1}{8}$ teaspoon paprika
$\frac{1}{2}$ cup light cream or half-and-half
Freshly ground white pepper to taste

FOR THE DUMPLINGS
2 cups flour
1 teaspoon salt
1 tablespoon baking powder
1 tablespoon vegetable shortening
$\frac{3}{4}$ cup milk

In a large covered soup pot or kettle, place the chicken. Add the onion, carrot, celery, and salt. Pour in enough water to cover and bring to a boil over high heat. Reduce the heat to medium low and simmer, partially covered, until the chicken is very tender, $1\frac{1}{2}$–2 hours.

Remove the chicken from the broth and cool. When cool enough to handle, remove all skin, bones, and gristle. Dice the chicken.

Strain the stock, discard the solids, and defat the stock. Measure 4 cups of the stock (reserve any extra for another use or, if necessary, add water to measure 4 cups).

In a large saucepan over medium-high heat, melt the butter. Stir in the flour and paprika. Stir until well blended and lemon colored, about 3 minutes. Pour in the 4 cups of stock, increase the heat to high, and bring to a boil, stirring often. Reduce the heat to medium low and cook, stirring, until the sauce is thickened and smooth, about 10 minutes. Add the diced chicken, cream or half-and-half, and white pepper. Season with additional salt and pepper if desired. Reduce the heat to medium low and cook slowly while preparing the dumplings.

Into a large bowl, sift the flour, salt, and baking powder. Blend in the shortening with a pastry blender or fork. Add the milk and mix well.

Dip a teaspoon into cold water and then into the dough. Spoon the dumplings on top of the gently bubbling chicken mixture. Cover and cook for 15 minutes without lifting the lid. Serve at once.

Chowning's Tavern Brunswick Stew

SERVES 8–10

The argument will never be settled as to whether this tasty dish came from Brunswick County, Virginia; Brunswick, Georgia; or Brunswick County, North Carolina, although Virginia's claim is the best documented. The recipe is now made with stewed chicken, corn, lima beans, and tomatoes and omits the squirrel, which was originally used.

2 chickens (about 3 pounds each), cut into 6 or 8 pieces
4–5 large tomatoes, peeled, seeded, and chopped, or 2 (16-ounce) cans, drained, seeded, and chopped
4 cups fresh or frozen corn kernels
3 medium all-purpose potatoes, peeled and cut into ½-inch dice

2 large onions, thinly sliced
2 cups fresh or frozen lima beans
2 cups fresh or frozen sliced okra
1 tablespoon salt, or to taste
1 tablespoon freshly ground black pepper, or to taste
1 teaspoon sugar, or to taste

In a large pot, place the chickens and add enough water to cover, 2–3 quarts. Bring to a boil over high heat. Reduce the heat to medium low and simmer, partially covered, until the chicken is falling off the bones and the broth is well flavored, 2–3 hours. Use a slotted spoon to transfer the chicken to a bowl and cool.

Skim the broth. Add the tomatoes, corn, potatoes, onions, lima beans, and okra. Season with the salt, pepper, and sugar. Bring to a simmer over medium heat. Reduce the heat to medium low and cook, stirring often, until the potatoes are tender, about 20 minutes.

Meanwhile, pull the chicken off the bones. Add the chicken to the vegetables and taste the stew for seasoning. Add more salt, pepper, or sugar as desired. Serve hot in warmed bowls.

SOUTHERN COOKS PRIZE OKRA FOR ITS DISTINCTIVE FLAVOR AND TEXTURE. THE VEGETABLE CAME TO THE NEW WORLD FROM AFRICA VIA THE SLAVE TRADE.

King's Arms Tavern Chicken Pot Pie

SERVES 8

FOR THE CHICKEN AND STOCK
2 broiler-fryers (2½–3 pounds each)
2 celery ribs, finely chopped
1 medium onion, sliced
1 bay leaf
1 teaspoon salt
½ teaspoon white pepper

FOR THE FILLING
½ cup (1 stick) unsalted butter
½ cup flour

1 (10-ounce) package frozen peas
4 celery ribs, sliced and cooked
4 carrots, sliced and cooked
2–3 medium all-purpose potatoes, diced
   and cooked
Salt and freshly ground white pepper

FOR ASSEMBLING THE PIES
1 large egg
2 tablespoons milk
2 recipes Pie Pastry (page 63)

In a large covered soup pot or kettle, place the chickens. Add the celery, onion, bay leaf, salt, and pepper. Pour in enough water to cover and bring to a boil over high heat. Reduce the heat to medium low and simmer, partially covered, until the chicken is very tender, 1½–2 hours. Skim the broth. Remove the chicken and cool.

When cool enough to handle, remove all skin, bones, and gristle from the chicken and cut into large pieces. Strain the broth and discard the solids.

In a large saucepan over medium-high heat, melt the butter. Add the flour and stir until well blended and lemon colored, about 3 minutes. Stirring constantly, pour in enough chicken stock to achieve the consistency of the sauce desired, about 4 cups. Reduce the heat to medium and simmer until thickened and smooth, about 5 minutes.

In a large bowl, combine the peas, celery, carrots, and potatoes. Add the chicken pieces and the sauce. Season with additional salt and pepper if desired. Stir gently to bind the ingredients, then set aside to cool.

Preheat the oven to 375°F. and butter eight 2-cup casseroles. Divide the vegetable and chicken mixture evenly among the casseroles. In a small bowl, beat the egg with the milk until blended. Roll out the pastry dough ⅛-inch thick. Cut out circles large enough to seal the edges to the rim to top each casserole. Use the tip of a sharp paring knife to cut a small hole in the center to allow the steam to escape. Prick the pastry with a fork and brush with the beaten egg. Bake until the crusts are golden brown and the filling is bubbling, 35–40 minutes. Serve piping hot.

Mrs. Vobe's Herb-Crusted Breast of Chicken with Smithfield Ham and Scuppernong Grape Sauce

SERVES 4

Mrs. Jane Vobe opened the King's Arms Tavern in 1772. Her name has lent itself to many tavern dishes over the years, the following being an excellent example. Scuppernongs are thick-skinned grapes found only in the South. As a substitute, use large red table grapes.

FOR THE SCUPPERNONG GRAPE SAUCE
1 cup Chicken Stock (page 24) or
   low-salt canned stock
½ cup orange juice
¼ cup scuppernong wine
¾ cup scuppernong grapes, seeded and
   skinned
¼ teaspoon sugar
⅛ teaspoon grated nutmeg
⅛ teaspoon cinnamon
1 tablespoon arrowroot
Salt and freshly ground black pepper to
   taste

FOR THE CHICKEN:
⅓ cup flour
⅓ cup fine cracker crumbs
1 teaspoon dried parsley flakes
1 teaspoon dried basil
½ teaspoon dried thyme
4 large boneless chicken breasts
   (6 ounces each)
Salt and freshly ground black pepper to
   taste
2 tablespoons (¼ stick) unsalted butter
2 tablespoons vegetable oil
4 thin slices Smithfield ham

To make the sauce, in a small saucepan, combine the chicken stock, orange juice, wine, grapes, sugar, nutmeg, and cinnamon. Bring to a boil over high heat, then reduce the heat to low. Mix the arrowroot in a small bowl with 1 teaspoon water. Slowly add this to the sauce, stirring constantly. Do not boil. Stir and heat the sauce until thickened, about 4 minutes. Strain the sauce and season with salt and pepper. Keep warm over low heat.

> FRESHLY GROUND NUTMEG ADDS JUST THE RIGHT NOTE OF FLAVOR TO THIS DISH. WHOLE NUTMEGS AND THE SMALL DEVICE ON WHICH TO GRATE THEM ARE SOLD IN THE STORES ON DUKE OF GLOUCESTER STREET IN WILLIAMSBURG.

To prepare the chicken, in a large shallow bowl, combine the flour, cracker crumbs, parsley flakes, basil, and thyme. Season the chicken breasts with salt and pepper. Roll the chicken in the cracker crumb mixture. In a large skillet over medium-high heat, melt the butter with the oil. Add the chicken and cook until golden brown, 3–5 minutes per side.

Place the ham in the center of 4 warmed serving plates. Arrange the chicken breasts on top and spoon over the hot scuppernong grape sauce. Serve immediately.

Ginger and Orange–Roasted Duck Breast

SERVES 4

FOR THE SAUCE

3 tablespoons sugar
¼ cup red wine vinegar
¼ cup orange juice
1 teaspoon ground ginger
1¾ cups Chicken Stock (page 24) or
  low-salt canned chicken stock, divided
2 tablespoons arrowroot
2 tablespoons Port
1 tablespoon grated orange peel

FOR THE DUCK

4 trimmed duck breasts with skin
  (6–8 ounces each)
Salt and freshly ground black pepper to
  taste
1 large onion, thinly sliced
Orange sections and finely chopped
  fresh parsley, for garnish

To make the sauce, in a small heavy saucepan, blend the sugar and vinegar. Cook over medium-high heat, swirling the pan often, until the sugar is melted. Increase the heat to high and boil until the mixture turns caramel brown, about 3–5 minutes. Remove from the heat and add the orange juice and ginger. Stir in half the chicken stock and return the pan to the heat. Heat gently over medium heat, stirring or whisking constantly until blended. In a small bowl, mix the arrowroot with the Port until the arrowroot has dissolved. Reduce the heat to low and stir in the arrowroot mixture. Add the orange peel and simmer gently for 3 minutes. Do not boil.

To cook the duck, preheat the oven to 400°F. In an ovenproof skillet large enough to hold them flat, place the breasts, skin side down. Season with salt and pepper and cook on top of the stove over medium-high heat, without turning, until the fat is rendered and the skin is golden brown, 5–7 minutes.

Remove the breasts and pour out the fat from the skillet. Add the onion and cook until slightly softened, about 2 minutes. Pour in the remaining chicken stock, increase the heat to high, and bring to a boil. Boil until the stock has reduced by half, 5–7 minutes. Return the breasts to the skillet, skin side up, season again with salt and pepper, and roast, uncovered, in the oven until firm to the touch, about 10 minutes. (Watch carefully and add 1–2 tablespoons of water at a time if necessary to prevent scorching.) Remove the duck to a work surface, cover loosely with foil, and let rest for 3 minutes.

Reheat the sauce gently over very low heat. Slice the breasts thickly, cutting against the grain, and arrange on a warmed platter. Garnish with orange sections and spoon over some of the sauce. Sprinkle with parsley and serve the remaining sauce on the side.

Ginger and Orange–Roasted Duck Breast

East India Company Fried Chicken

SERVES 12

This recipe commemorates Great Britain's trading interests in India. The chicken is spiced
with cinnamon, a spice long associated with the exotic Far East.

2 broiler-fryers (3–3½ pounds each)   1 teaspoon salt
1 cup flour   ⅛ teaspoon freshly ground white pepper
4 large eggs   1 teaspoon cinnamon
4 cups fresh bread crumbs   Vegetable oil for frying

Cut each chicken into 8 pieces. In a large bowl, place the flour. In a separate bowl, beat
the eggs with 2 tablespoons water. In a third bowl, mix the bread crumbs with the salt,
pepper, and cinnamon.

Roll the chicken in the flour to coat thoroughly. Dip in the egg mixture, then
lightly in the bread crumbs. Dip in the egg mixture again, then lightly in the bread
crumbs. Place the chicken on baking sheets and refrigerate for 1 hour.

In 2 large deep electric skillets, heat 1¼ inches of oil to 375°F. (Alternatively, use 2
nonelectric skillets and a thermometer.) Fry the pieces of chicken for 3 minutes. Turn
each piece over with kitchen tongs. Fry for 3 minutes and turn again. Continue frying
and turning each piece every 5 minutes until the chicken is tender, 12–15 minutes
total. Do not overcook. Drain on paper towels.

King's Arms Tavern Colonial Game Pie

SERVES 8

This classic King's Arms favorite is made of venison, duck, rabbit, and rich brown sauce laced with currant jelly, all beneath a crusty pastry top.

1 duck (4–5 pounds)
Salt and freshly ground black pepper to taste
1 rabbit (2–2½ pounds), cut into 8 pieces
1 pound fillet or shoulder of venison, trimmed and cut into ½-inch cubes
¼ cup vegetable oil
1 cup Port
3 cups Brown Sauce (recipe follows)
1 clove garlic, minced

1 tablespoon Worcestershire sauce
½ cup seedless currant jelly
½ pound sliced bacon, cut into 1-inch pieces
10 ounces mushrooms, cleaned, trimmed, and halved or quartered
1 (10-ounce) package frozen pearl onions, thawed
1 large egg
2 tablespoons milk
2 recipes Pie Pastry (page 63)

Preheat the oven to 400°F. Season the duck inside and out with salt and pepper. On a rack in a large roasting pan, place the duck breast side up. Roast for 30 minutes, reduce the temperature to 325°F., and roast until the juices run clear when pierced with a fork at the thickest part of the thigh, or 20–22 minutes per pound. Remove from the pan and cool.

In a large covered casserole or Dutch oven, place the rabbit. Pour in enough water to barely cover the bottom of the casserole. Season with salt and pepper. Cover and cook over medium heat, turning the pieces often, until tender, about 1 hour. Add small amounts of water if necessary to prevent scorching. Remove the rabbit from the casserole and cool.

Season the venison with salt and pepper. In a large skillet over high heat, heat the oil. Add the venison and cook, stirring often, until the cubes are lightly browned on all sides, about 5 minutes. Remove the venison to a plate or platter and pour off the fat from the skillet. Pour the Port into the skillet and return to the heat. Cook, stirring to scrape up any browned bits in the bottom of the pan, until the Port has reduced by half, about 5 minutes. Return the venison to the skillet and pour in the brown sauce. Reduce the heat to medium low, cover, and simmer until the venison is very tender, about 30–45 minutes for fillet or 60 minutes for shoulder. Stir occasionally.

Meanwhile, remove all skin, bones, and gristle from the duck and the rabbit. Cut the duck and rabbit into 1½–2-inch pieces and add to the skillet with the venison. Season the mixture with the garlic and Worcestershire sauce. Stir in the currant jelly and season with salt and pepper. Remove from the heat and cool completely. (The recipe can be prepared ahead up to this point. It keeps refrigerated for up to 3 days or frozen for up to 1 month.)

In a large skillet over medium-high heat, fry the bacon until crisp, 3–5 minutes. Using a slotted spoon, remove the bacon and drain on paper towels. Pour off all but 2 tablespoons of fat from the skillet. Return the skillet to the heat and add the mushrooms. Cook, stirring often, until softened and lightly browned, about 7–10 minutes. Pat dry the onions.

Divide the venison mixture into 8 (2-cup capacity) individual greased casserole dishes. Add equal amounts of the mushrooms, bacon, and onions. In a small bowl, mix the egg and milk to make an egg wash.

Preheat the oven to 375°F. Roll out the pastry to a thickness of ⅛ inch. Cut out circles large enough to seal the edges to the rim to top each casserole. Use the tip of a sharp paring knife to cut a small hole in the center to allow the steam to escape. Prick the pastry with a fork and brush with the egg wash. Bake at 350°F. for 25–30 minutes, or until the crust is golden brown. Serve piping hot.

Brown Sauce

MAKES 1 QUART

¼ cup (½ stick) unsalted butter
1 cup flour
½ cup tomato puree
2 quarts hot Beef Stock (page 29) or
  low-salt canned beef stock
1 tablespoon powdered beef bouillon or
  1 beef bouillon cube

1 tablespoon bottled brown gravy
  sauce
Salt and freshly ground black pepper to
  taste
Caramel color (optional)

In a large saucepan over medium-high heat, melt the butter. Add the flour and stir until the mixture is lightly browned. Stir in the tomato puree, beef stock, and bouillon. Increase the heat to high and bring to a boil, stirring often, until the mixture is smooth and slightly thickened, about 15 minutes. Reduce the heat to very low and simmer, stirring occasionally, until the sauce has reduced by half, about 2 hours.

Add the bottled brown gravy sauce, season with salt and pepper, and add the caramel coloring, if desired. Strain through a fine-mesh sieve and cool. Refrigerate until ready to use.

Chowning's Tavern Roast Game Hens
with White Wine Mushroom Sauce

SERVES 4

½ cup (1 stick) plus 2 tablespoons softened unsalted butter, divided
½ pound small mushrooms, trimmed and quartered
¼ cup flour
2 cups Chicken Stock (page 24) or low-salt canned chicken stock

½ cup dry white wine, preferably from Burgundy
Salt and freshly ground black pepper to taste
1 tablespoon finely chopped parsley
4 game hens (1¼ pounds each)

Preheat the oven to 450°F., lightly oil a rack, and set it in a large roasting pan.

In a large skillet over medium-high heat, melt ¼ cup butter. Add the mushrooms and cook, stirring often, until well browned, about 10 minutes. Using a slotted spoon, transfer the mushrooms to drain on paper towels. In the skillet over medium-high heat, melt ¼ cup butter. Add the flour and stir until well blended and lemon colored, about 3 minutes. Pour in the chicken stock, increase the heat to high, and bring to a boil, stirring often. Reduce the heat to medium and simmer until thick and creamy, about 5 minutes. Stir in the wine, add the mushrooms, and simmer 5 minutes longer. Season with salt and pepper. Stir in the parsley. Reheat over low heat before serving if made in advance.

Rub the game hens with the remaining 2 tablespoons softened butter. Season well with salt and pepper. Arrange, breast side up, on the oiled rack and reduce the oven temperature to 350°F. Roast the game hens, basting often, until golden brown and the juices run clear when pierced at the thickest part of the thigh, about 45 minutes–1 hour. Let sit, loosely covered with foil, for about 10 minutes before serving.

Place the hens on individual plates and spoon over a small amount of the sauce. Serve the remaining sauce on the side.

Roast Quail with Corn Bread Stuffing

SERVES 4–6

Quail are often sold partially boned. This means that all but the leg bones have been removed to facilitate cooking and eating. If using fresh quail, ask your butcher to bone the birds. To do it yourself, cut away the backbone and remove the ribs, breastbone, and wishbone. Cut each bird in half lengthwise, leaving in the leg and thigh bone.

2 tablespoons (¼ stick) unsalted butter
2 tablespoons vegetable oil
1 large onion, finely chopped
1 celery rib, thinly sliced
2 cups crumbled day-old corn bread
2 cups day-old French or Italian bread, torn into 1-inch pieces

1 cup finely chopped pecans
½ cup Chicken Stock (page 24) or low-salt canned chicken stock
Salt and freshly ground black pepper to taste
12 small quail, partially boned
12 strips lean bacon

Preheat the oven to 425°F. and butter a large baking dish.

In a large heavy saucepan over medium-high heat, melt the butter and oil. Add the onion and celery. Cook, stirring often, until softened, 3–5 minutes. Stir in the corn bread, bread, and pecans. Remove from the heat and pour in just enough of the chicken stock to moisten the stuffing without rendering it too mushy. Season well with salt and pepper.

Working with one quail at a time, season the cavity with salt and pepper. Fill each cavity with 1–2 tablespoons of the stuffing. Use a trussing needle and kitchen thread (butcher's twine) to secure both openings of the quail. Into a small buttered baking dish, spoon the leftover stuffing.

Wrap each quail with a strip of bacon. In the large baking dish, arrange each quail, breast side up. Sprinkle with salt and pepper and roast until the juices run clean when a thigh is pierced with the tip of a small knife, 30–35 minutes. Place the dish of leftover stuffing in the oven during the last 15 minutes of cooking.

Remove the trussing strings from the quail and serve on a warmed platter with the extra stuffing on the side.

Roast Duck with Fruit Stuffing

SERVES 4

Ducks were plentiful in early Virginia, and hunting was an important way of supplying food. Colonial cooks lost no time learning to stuff and roast mallards, black ducks, teals, and widgeons. In this recipe, the fruit softens as the hot juices bathe the cavity. Use a green apple and top-quality dried apricots for best results.

¼ cup (½ stick) unsalted butter
1 small onion, finely chopped
4 cups day-old white bread cubes
Salt
Freshly ground black pepper
1 large apple, preferably Granny Smith, peeled, cubed, and cut into ½-inch cubes

4–5 dried apricots, finely chopped
¼ cup raisins or currants
1 large egg, lightly beaten
½ cup orange juice
1 duck (5–6 pounds)

To prepare the stuffing, in a large skillet over medium-high heat, melt the butter. Add the onion and cook, stirring often, until softened, 3–5 minutes. Add the bread cubes and toss well to mix. Transfer to a large bowl and sprinkle over ½ teaspoon salt and ¼ teaspoon pepper. Add the apple, apricots, and raisins or currants to the bowl. Toss again to mix.

In a small bowl, beat the egg with the orange juice. Pour over the stuffing mixture and gently stir to combine.

Preheat the oven to 400°F. Season the inside of the duck cavity with salt and pepper. Fill the cavity loosely with the stuffing and close the opening with small skewers (see Note). Attach the neck skin to the back of the duck with a skewer. Place, breast side up, on a rack set in a large roasting pan. Roast for 20 minutes, prick the skin all over, and reduce the oven temperature to 350°F. Continue to roast until golden brown and the juices run clear, not pink, when pierced at the thickest part of the thigh, about 15 minutes per pound. Let sit, covered loosely with foil, for 10–15 minutes before carving.

NOTE: Place any leftover stuffing in a buttered casserole. Bake in the oven with the duck for the last 20 minutes of the roasting time.

Pan-Fried Rabbit

SERVES 4

This is an excellent dish to serve those who are unfamiliar with rabbit. Long, slow cooking brings out the tender lean moistness similar to dark-meat chicken.

1 rabbit (2–2½ pounds), cut into
  8 pieces
½ cup flour
Salt
Freshly ground black pepper
4 tablespoons (½ stick) unsalted butter,
  divided

2 tablespoons vegetable oil
1 cup Port
2 medium onions, thinly sliced
2 medium carrots, peeled and thinly
  sliced

In a large pot, place the rabbit and pour in enough cold water to cover. Bring to a boil over high heat. Reduce the heat to medium and simmer, partially covered, until the rabbit is tender, about 30 minutes. Remove the rabbit to cool on a large platter. Reserve the cooking liquid.

In a large shallow bowl, mix the flour with 1 teaspoon salt and ½ teaspoon pepper. Pat the rabbit dry and add to the flour mixture. Turn to coat on all sides and shake off any excess flour. In a large heavy skillet over medium-high heat, melt 2 tablespoons of the butter with the oil. Add the rabbit and cook, turning often, until browned on all sides, about 10 minutes. Remove to a platter and cover with foil to keep warm.

Pour off the fat from the skillet. Add the Port and increase the heat to high. Bring to a boil, stirring to scrape up any browned bits in the bottom of the skillet. Pour in 1 cup of the reserved cooking liquid (add more if necessary–the liquid should barely cover the rabbit in the skillet). Return the rabbit to the skillet and reduce the heat to medium. Simmer, uncovered, until the rabbit is falling off the bones, 30–35 minutes.

Meanwhile, in a large nonstick skillet over medium-high heat, melt the remaining 2 tablespoons of butter. Add the onions and carrots. Cook, stirring often, until just tender, 10–15 minutes. Season with salt and pepper.

Transfer the rabbit to a warmed serving platter. Bring the cooking juices to a boil and cook until reduced and thickened, 5 minutes. Pour the sauce over the rabbit and garnish with the onions and carrots.

Roast Turkey with Sausage, Apple, and Pecan Dressing

SERVES 8–12

Wealthy Virginia planter William Byrd, writing early in the eighteenth century,
described a "large fat turkey-hen which weighs from thirty or forty and even more pounds."
While this makes a good story, the turkeys colonists consumed were generally
smaller than these huge specimens and were often stewed rather than roasted.
The dressing features sausage, apples, and pecans.

FOR THE DRESSING
1 pound bulk fresh mild or hot sausage
2 large onions, finely chopped
2 celery ribs, finely chopped
3 cups cooked corn bread, cut into
　½-inch dice
2 cups day-old French or Italian bread,
　crusts removed and cut into ½-inch
　dice
2 large cooking apples, preferably
　Granny Smith, peeled, cored, and cut
　into ½-inch dice
1½ cups chopped pecans
½ cup (1 stick) unsalted butter, melted

2 tablespoons finely chopped fresh
　parsley
1 teaspoon salt
½ teaspoon freshly ground black pepper

FOR THE TURKEY
1 trimmed turkey (12–14 pounds)
Salt and freshly ground black pepper to
　taste
¼ cup (½ stick) unsalted butter, softened
3 tablespoons flour
1½ cups turkey stock, Chicken Stock
　(page 24), or low-salt canned chicken
　stock

To prepare the dressing, in a large skillet over medium-high heat, place the sausage and cook, stirring often, until no trace of pink remains. Use a slotted spoon to transfer the sausage to drain on paper towels. Pour off all but 1 tablespoon of the fat from the skillet. Add the onions and celery to the skillet and cook, stirring often, until softened, about 5 minutes. In a large bowl, combine the drained sausage, onions, celery, corn bread, day-old bread, apples, and pecans. Stir in the melted butter, parsley, salt, and pepper.

Dry the turkey inside and out with paper towels. Season the inside of the cavity with salt and pepper. Fill the breast and neck cavities with the dressing. Truss the turkey securely with a trussing needle and kitchen string.

Preheat the oven to 400°F. Rub the turkey with the butter and season well with salt and pepper. In a large roasting pan, place the bird on its side. Cook for 15 minutes, then turn on the other side for 15 minutes. Turn, breast side down, in the pan and cook until the back is golden brown, about 30 minutes. Reduce the oven temperature to 325°F. and turn, breast side up. Continue to roast for 18 minutes per pound, basting every 20 minutes, until a meat thermometer inserted into the thickest part of the thigh registers 180°F. Transfer the turkey to a warmed platter and let sit, loosely covered with foil, for 10–15 minutes.

Skim the fat from the surface of the roasting pan juices. Pour off the clear juices and reserve. Place the roasting pan on top of the stove and sprinkle over the flour. Cook over medium-high heat, stirring constantly, until the flour is lightly browned, 2–3 minutes. Pour in the turkey or chicken stock and increase the heat to high. Stir or whisk constantly until the gravy comes to a boil. Reduce the heat to low and simmer for 5 minutes. Add the reserved clear pan juices and season with salt and pepper. Strain through a sieve and pour into a warmed gravy boat. Carve the turkey and pass the gravy on the side.

Turkey and Cranberry Hash

SERVES 6–8

"Hash," from the French verb hacher *(to chop), makes the most of Thanksgiving Day leftovers. Here, turkey and cranberries are held together with gravy and browned until crisp. Serve in wedges with poached eggs for an after-the-big-day brunch.*

2 tablespoons (¼ stick) unsalted
  butter
1 onion, finely chopped
1 celery rib, finely chopped
1 pound cooked skinless turkey, white
  and dark meat combined, cut into
  ½-inch cubes

½ cup chopped fresh cranberries or
  ¼ cup dried cranberries soaked in
  white wine
¼ cup leftover turkey gravy or heavy
  cream
Salt and freshly ground black pepper to
  taste
Snipped fresh chives, for garnish

In a large skillet with sloping sides over medium-high heat, melt the butter. Add the onion and celery. Cook, stirring often, until softened, 3–5 minutes. Add the turkey, cranberries, and gravy. Season with salt and pepper and reduce the heat to medium. Cover and cook until the bottom is crusty brown, 20–25 minutes. Slip out onto a plate and carefully flip to the other side. Cook, uncovered, until golden brown on the other side, about 15 minutes. Slide out onto a work surface and sprinkle with chives. Cut into wedges and serve.

Beef, Lamb,
Pork,
and Veal

THE "better sort" in colonial Virginia ate meat daily, especially for the midday meal, at which they often had a choice of several kinds of beef, lamb, pork, or veal, game, poultry, and fish. Slaves and poor whites, whose diets were based on corn, consumed meat only occasionally.

Although archaeological evidence from house and tavern sites shows that early Virginians primarily favored beef (which is not surprising since the majority of settlers in eastern Virginia came from England), it was pork that travelers extolled. "Their pork is famous, whole Virginia shoots [young hogs] being frequently barbecued in England; their bacon is excellent, the hams being scarce to be distinguished from those of Westphalia," wrote Hugh Jones, who published a guide to Virginia upon his return to England in the 1720s.

To keep meat from spoiling in the days before refrigeration and canning, colonial housewives pickled, corned, smoked, dried, and potted meats for later consumption. Salting was the most popular way to preserve meat. A French traveler observed that Virginians ate large quantities of salted pork: "The people here have a special way of curing [hams] that consists of salting and smoking almost as we do in France; however, ours cannot touch theirs for flavor and quality. The summer heat here restricts them to this diet, for fresh-killed meat must be consumed within twenty-four hours or else it will spoil." So hogs were slaughtered only in the winter and fresh pork seldom was served.

The production of Virginia hams has long been concentrated near Williamsburg in Suffolk and Surry Counties where settlers' hogs foraged for mast (native berries, nuts, and roots). Unlike the brine-cured hams sold in supermarkets, country hams receive a dry rub of nitrates and salt or salt and sugar or molasses. After several weeks of curing, the hams are hung, hocks down, to preserve their juices and smoked over smoldering hickory. Then they age in the smokehouse for months or sometimes years. The result? A flavorful Virginia ham to be savored by those who truly appreciate exceptional taste.

PREVIOUS PAGES FROM LEFT: Corn Bread, Collard Greens, Glazed Roast Loin of Pork, and Hoppin' John.

Oven-Braised Gingered Pot Roast

SERVES 4–6

Double the amount of beef stock if you can't find strong ginger beer.
Serve with caramelized onions and glazed carrots.

1 3-inch piece fresh ginger (2 ounces), peeled
1 whole chuck roast (3 pounds)
2 tablespoons (¼ stick) unsalted butter
2 tablespoons vegetable oil
Salt and freshly ground black pepper to taste
2 carrots, peeled and coarsely chopped

1 onion, coarsely chopped
1 celery rib, thickly sliced
2 tablespoons flour
1 cup dark strong ginger beer
1 cup Beef Stock (page 29) or low-salt canned beef stock
¼ teaspoon ground ginger, or more to taste

Cut the ginger in half and set one half aside. Cut the other half into slivers ⅛-inch thick and about 1-inch long. Using a small paring knife, make deep slits in the beef at 1-inch intervals. Fill each slit with a sliver of ginger. Wrap in plastic and refrigerate for at least 1 day or up to 3 days.

Preheat the oven to 350°F. In a large skillet over medium-high heat, melt the butter with the oil. Season the beef with salt and pepper. Add the beef to the skillet and cook, turning often, until lightly browned on all sides, about 5 minutes. Remove to a plate and pour off all but 1 tablespoon of fat from the skillet. Return the skillet to the heat and add the carrots, onion, and celery. Coarsely chop the remaining half of the peeled ginger and add to the skillet. Cook, stirring often, until the vegetables and ginger are slightly softened, 3–5 minutes. Stir in the flour and cook 2 minutes longer. Pour in the ginger beer and the stock. Increase the heat to high and bring the mixture to a boil, stirring often.

In a covered ovenproof casserole or Dutch oven, place the browned beef. Pour the boiling mixture from the skillet over the beef. Cover tightly and place in the oven. Cook, turning occasionally and basting often, until the beef is very tender, about 2 hours.

Remove the beef to a platter and cover with foil. Into a large heavy saucepan, strain the sauce from the casserole. Bring to a boil over medium-high heat and season well with salt, pepper, and the ground ginger. Boil, whisking often, until the sauce is thick enough to coat the back of a spoon, about 5 minutes. Check for seasoning and add salt, pepper, and ground ginger to taste.

Slice the beef against the grain and place on a warmed serving dish. Pour the sauce over and serve at once.

Standing Rib Roast with Yorkshire Pudding

SERVES 8–10

1 beef rib roast with bones
   (10–12 pounds)
Salt and freshly ground black pepper to
   taste

½ cup Beef Stock (page 29), low-salt
   canned beef broth, or water
1 recipe Yorkshire Pudding (recipe
   follows)
Bottled horseradish

Preheat the oven to 350°F. Rub the top (or fat) side of the beef with plenty of salt and pepper. In a large roasting pan, stand the roast fat side up. Roast, basting often, until a meat thermometer inserted into the center of the flesh reads 130°F. for rare, 140°F. for medium, and 160°F. for well done. Count on about 18 minutes roasting time per pound for rare.

Remove the roast to a carving board and cover loosely with foil. Drain off the fat and place the roasting pan on top of the stove. Pour in the beef stock and bring to a boil over high heat, stirring constantly to scrape the roasting bits from the bottom of the pan. Season with salt and pepper. Carve the roast into thick slices and spoon the pan juices over. Serve with Yorkshire pudding and horseradish.

Yorkshire Pudding

SERVES 8

Yorkshire pudding is the quintessential part of an English roast beef dinner. Made from an egg batter and baked in a heavy skillet, it is one of those dishes that is simple yet demanding in its execution. The skillet must be very hot and the top of the pudding must be crispy brown. Lard or butter can be used as a substitute but neither gives the flavor of the drippings.

2 large eggs, lightly beaten
1 cup milk
1 cup flour
Pinch grated nutmeg

Salt and freshly ground black pepper
to taste
½ cup melted beef drippings, lard, or
butter, divided

In a large bowl, beat the eggs with the milk. Whisk in the flour and season with the nutmeg and salt and pepper. Stir in half of the melted drippings or fat. Let stand at room temperature for 30 minutes.

TOAD-IN-THE-HOLE, ANOTHER BRITISH FAVORITE, CONSISTS OF SMALL COOKED LINK SAUSAGES BAKED IN YORKSHIRE PUDDING BATTER.

Preheat the oven to 425°F. In a small ovenproof skillet, place the remaining drippings or fat. Place the skillet in the oven. When the skillet is sizzling hot, pour in the batter. Bake until puffed and lightly browned, about 30 minutes. Reduce the heat to 350°F. and bake until well browned and crisp on top, 10–15 minutes. Cut into large squares and serve hot.

Steak and Kidney Pie

SERVES 4–6

Kidneys, a rich and flavorful source of protein, were heartily enjoyed by the colonists and their British cousins. Most European diets then as now featured a variety of items collectively called offal–calf's head, oxtail, heart, and kidney. One of the most popular English pub offerings has always been the classic steak and kidney pie.

¾ pound top sirloin of beef, cut into 1-inch cubes
½ pound lamb, beef, or veal kidneys, cut into 1-inch pieces
½ teaspoon salt
¼ teaspoon freshly ground black pepper
¼ teaspoon paprika
¼ cup flour
1 medium onion, thinly sliced

2 tablespoons vegetable shortening
2 cups Beef Stock (page 29) or low-salt canned beef stock
1 bay leaf
2 tablespoons (¼ stick) unsalted butter
4 medium mushrooms, trimmed and thinly sliced
2 hard-cooked eggs, sliced
1 recipe Pie Pastry (page 63)

Trim the sirloin and kidneys of excess fat. Cut the kidneys into ⅛-inch-thick slices.

Put the salt, pepper, paprika, and flour in a paper bag and shake well. Add the beef, kidneys, and onion to the bag and shake until well coated.

In a large covered skillet or Dutch oven over medium-high heat, melt the shortening. Add the beef, kidneys, and onion. Cook, stirring often, until the meat is well browned, 7–10 minutes. Pour in the beef stock and add the bay leaf. Reduce the heat to low, cover the skillet, and simmer until the beef is tender, about 1 hour. Remove and discard the bay leaf. Transfer the meat mixture to a 1½-quart baking dish and cool.

> THE RECIPE FOR THIS TRADITIONAL BRITISH FAVORITE CALLS FOR COOKING THE FILLING SEPARATELY UNTIL THE MEAT IS TENDER, THEN ADDING THE PASTRY AND BAKING AGAIN UNTIL THE CRUST IS BROWN. POTATOES ARE OFTEN ADDED.

In a small skillet over medium-high heat, melt the butter. Add the mushrooms and cook, stirring often, until softened, about 5 minutes. Top the meat mixture with the mushrooms and sliced eggs.

Preheat the oven to 450°F. Roll the pastry out into a shape large enough to cover the baking dish by 1 inch. Cover the pie, sealing the sides, and cut vents for the steam to escape. Bake for 10–15 minutes, then reduce the heat to 350°F. and bake for an additional 15–20 minutes, or until the crust is golden brown.

King's Arms Tavern Filet Mignon Stuffed with Oysters

SERVES 6

If the filets are being prepared in advance, drain and cool the oysters before stuffing.

6 1½-inch-thick beef tenderloin filets
   (6–8 ounces each)
12 medium shucked oysters
Salt and freshly ground black pepper to
   taste

3 tablespoons unsalted butter, divided
6 slices bacon
1 teaspoon finely chopped fresh parsley

Insert a sharp knife into the side of each filet. With a short sawing motion, make a deep pocket without puncturing the opposite side.

Season the oysters with salt and pepper. In a small skillet over medium-high heat, melt 1 tablespoon of the butter. Add the oysters and cook only until the edges begin to curl, 1–2 minutes. Drain on paper towels.

Stuff each filet with 2 oysters. Wrap a slice of bacon around each filet and secure with a toothpick. Broil or sauté to the desired doneness, 5–7 minutes on each side for medium rare.

In a small saucepan, heat the remaining butter until lightly browned. Stir in the parsley and pour over the cooked filets.

Chowning's Tavern Ploughman's Pasty

SERVES 4

Farm workers used to carry a savory pie in their pocket for lunch.
This modern version is best eaten right out of the oven.

1 recipe Pie Pastry (page 63)
½ pound thinly sliced turkey breast
¼ pound thinly sliced Virginia ham
4 thin slices Swiss cheese
¼ head green cabbage, thinly shredded

4 tablespoons Red Pepper Relish
  (page 55)
Salt and freshly ground black pepper to
  taste
1 large egg
1 tablespoon milk

Cut the dough into 4 pieces and roll each piece into a 7-inch circle. Place the circles on a large baking sheet and chill for 20 minutes.

Preheat the oven to 400°F.

Working on a lightly floured surface, place equal amounts of the turkey, ham, and cheese on one half of each circle, leaving a ½-inch border. Add one quarter of the shredded cabbage and 1 tablespoon red pepper relish, and season with salt and pepper. Fold the pastry over the filling to form a half-moon shape. Pinch the edges with the tines of a fork to seal. Carefully place each pasty on a large baking sheet.

In a small bowl, beat the egg with the milk and a pinch of salt. Brush the pasties with a small amount of this egg wash. Bake for about 45 minutes, or until the pasties are golden brown. Serve warm.

IN MEDIEVAL ENGLAND, A PASTY WAS A LARGE, ELABORATE CONCOCTION OF MEAT, POULTRY, OR FISH BAKED IN A THICK DOUGH. ONE RECIPE INSTRUCTED THE COOK TO STUFF A PARTRIDGE WITH A PIGEON, A FOWL WITH THE PARTRIDGE, A GOOSE WITH THE FOWL, AND FINALLY A TURKEY WITH THE GOOSE, ALL TO BE BAKED IN A CASE MADE FROM A BUSHEL OF FLOUR AND TEN POUNDS OF BUTTER. PASTIES HAVE SHRUNK OVER TIME, AND NOW THE WORD DESCRIBES INDIVIDUAL TURNOVERS FILLED WITH CHOPPED MEAT OR FISH AND VEGETABLES.

Braised Short Ribs of Beef

SERVES 4

¼ cup flour
Salt
Freshly ground black pepper to taste
4 meaty short ribs of beef (3–4 pounds
  total)
2 tablespoons (¼ stick) unsalted butter
1 small onion, finely chopped

1 medium carrot, peeled and finely
  chopped
1 celery rib, finely chopped
2 tablespoons vegetable shortening
2 cups Brown Sauce (page 109)
¼ cup red wine

Preheat the oven to 300°F. In a large shallow bowl, combine the flour, 1 teaspoon salt, and pepper. Add the ribs and turn to coat on all sides.

In a large, heavy skillet over medium-high heat, melt the butter. Add the onion, carrot, and celery. Cook until softened, stirring often, about 5 minutes. Transfer the vegetables to a heavy covered ovenproof casserole.

In the skillet over medium-high heat, melt the shortening. Add the ribs and cook on all sides until well browned, 5–7 minutes. Transfer to the casserole.

Heat the brown sauce to boiling and pour into the casserole. Cover and bake until the meat is very tender, about 2½ hours. Remove the ribs and cover to keep warm.

Skim off the fat from the sauce and strain. Adjust the seasoning and stir in the wine. Return the ribs to the sauce and heat on top of the stove for 5–10 minutes before serving.

Virginia Ham with Brandied Peaches

1 Virginia ham (10–12 pounds)
2 tablespoons packed light brown sugar
1 tablespoon bread crumbs
1 teaspoon ground cloves

3 tablespoons honey, dry sherry, or
  sweet-pickle vinegar
Brandied Peaches (recipe follows),
  spiced crab apples, or any spiced fruit

To cook a Virginia ham, scrub the ham to remove the coating of seasonings and cover with water. Soak for 24 hours, changing the water often.

In a large covered roasting pan, place the ham, skin side down, with enough fresh water to cover. Bring to a boil, reduce the heat, and simmer, covered, for 20–25 minutes per pound. When cooked, skin the ham and trim off the excess fat. These directions apply to a Virginia ham that has been cured for at least 12 months. If the ham has been cured less than 12 months, follow the instructions on the wrapper or hang the ham and allow it to age.

To finish the ham, preheat the oven to 375°F. In a small bowl, combine the brown sugar, bread crumbs, and cloves. Press this mixture into the ham.

In a shallow baking pan, place the ham and bake for 15 minutes, or until the sugar melts.

Remove the ham from the oven and drizzle honey, sherry, or sweet-pickle vinegar over it. Return to the oven for 15 minutes.

Serve garnished with brandied peaches or any spiced fruit.

> "To eat the Ham in Perfection steep it in Half Milk and half water for Thirty-six hours, and then having brought the Water to a Boil put the Ham therein and let it Simmer, not boil, for 4 to 5 Hours according to size of the Ham— *for simmering brings the Salt out* and boiling drives it in."
>
> *This recipe is written on the flyleaf of a Bible that belonged to Colonel William Byrd of Westover plantation, one of the wealthiest and most influential Virginians of his time.*

Brandied Peaches

MAKES 1 QUART

2 (1-pound, 13-ounce) cans peach halves
½ cup sugar

½ cup brandy, preferably peach or fruit brandy
3–4 drops almond extract

Drain the peaches and reserve 1 cup of the juice. In a small saucepan, boil the reserved peach juice until it is reduced to ½ cup. Add the sugar and brandy. Mix well and add the almond extract. Cool.

Pour the brandy syrup over the peaches and serve, or pack the peaches in a sterilized 1-quart glass jar, add the brandy syrup, and seal according to the manufacturer's directions.

Chowning's Tavern Barbecued Ribs of Shoat with Barbecue Sauce

SERVES 6–8

"Shoat" is an old English word for a young weaned pig.

¼ cup sugar
¼ cup coarse salt
1 teaspoon allspice
1 teaspoon freshly ground black pepper
1 teaspoon ginger

½ teaspoon cinnamon
½ teaspoon cayenne pepper
6 pounds lean spareribs, cut into sections
1 recipe Barbecue Sauce (recipe follows)

In a small bowl, mix together the sugar, salt, allspice, black pepper, ginger, cinnamon, and cayenne pepper. Use your fingers to rub the mixture into the spareribs, thoroughly coating all surfaces. Wrap each section in plastic and refrigerate overnight.

Build a charcoal fire with a drip pan placed in the center. Oil the grates and let the coals burn to a gray ash. Cook the ribs on the grill, turning often, about 1 hour. Begin to brush and baste the ribs with the barbecue sauce, turning them every 10 minutes, for 45 minutes. Check to see if the ribs are thoroughly cooked by pulling apart one of the sections. If the ribs do not separate easily, cover with foil and check again after 15 minutes. Cut the ribs into individual pieces and serve.

Barbecue Sauce

MAKES 2 CUPS

2 cups ketchup
1 cup distilled white vinegar
½ cup packed dark brown sugar
1 large onion, finely chopped

2 cloves garlic, minced
2 tablespoons Worcestershire sauce
½ teaspoon Tabasco sauce
Salt and freshly ground black pepper

In a large nonreactive saucepan, combine the ketchup, vinegar, brown sugar, onion, garlic, Worcestershire sauce, Tabasco sauce, and salt and pepper and bring to a boil over high heat. Reduce the heat to medium low and simmer, partially covered, stirring often, until thickened and dark colored, about 30 minutes. Strain and cool to room temperature.

Glazed Roast Loin of Pork

SERVES 6

Serve with cinnamon-flavored baked apples or homemade applesauce.

FOR THE APPLE BRANDY GLAZE
1 cup packed dark brown sugar
1 tablespoon dry mustard
1 teaspoon salt
¼ teaspoon freshly ground black pepper
⅛ teaspoon cloves
⅛ teaspoon allspice
¼ cup apple brandy

FOR THE APPLE BRANDY SAUCE
¾ cup apple jelly
1 teaspoon grated lemon peel
2 tablespoons lemon juice

½ small onion, grated
⅛ teaspoon ginger
1 teaspoon bottled horseradish, drained
½ cup apple brandy

FOR THE ROAST
1 whole pork loin (6 pounds), with the
    chine bone separated (not removed
    entirely) from the bone, at room
    temperature
1 teaspoon salt
½ teaspoon freshly ground black pepper

To prepare the glaze, in a small bowl, combine the brown sugar, mustard, salt, pepper, cloves, allspice, and apple brandy. Mix well.

To make the sauce, in a small saucepan, combine the apple jelly, lemon peel, lemon juice, onion, ginger, horseradish, and brandy. Warm over low heat until the jelly has dissolved. Cool and set aside.

To roast the pork, rub the loin with the salt and pepper.

Preheat the oven to 350°F. On an oiled rack in a large roasting pan, place the pork. Roast until the internal temperature registers at least 165°F. on a meat thermometer, 2–2½ hours.

Thirty minutes before the end of the roasting time, skim and discard the fat from the roasting pan, leaving the drippings. Brush the pork several times with the glaze during the last ½ hour of cooking. Transfer the roast to a platter and cover with foil to keep warm.

Skim off and discard all the fat from the pan, leaving the drippings. Set the pan on top of the stove and pour in the sauce. Bring to a boil over high heat, stirring to pick up any roasting bits in the bottom of the pan. Taste for seasoning and strain into a warmed sauceboat. Cut the loin into thick slices and pass the sauce on the side.

Lamb Stew

SERVES 6

*After colonists brought sheep to the New World, lamb and mutton became
commonplace. Mutton was most likely used in stews like the one that follows.
Sadly, true mutton with its earthy and gamy flavor is almost impossible to find these days.
Good lamb is readily available, however, and with a little loving care you can
prepare a stew that rivals those of long ago.*

2 pounds lean shoulder of lamb, cut into
1½-inch cubes

Salt and freshly ground black pepper to
taste

1 cup flour

2 tablespoons (¼ stick) unsalted butter

2 tablespoons vegetable oil

2 cups Beef Stock (page 29) or low-salt
canned beef stock

2 large carrots, peeled and cut into
½-inch cubes

2 medium all-purpose potatoes, peeled
and cut into ½-inch cubes

1 large white turnip, peeled and cut into
½-inch cubes

1 large onion, thinly sliced

Preheat the oven to 350°F. Trim the lamb of all fat and pat dry with paper towels. Season well on all sides with salt and pepper. Dredge the lamb in the flour and shake off any excess flour.

In a large skillet over medium-high heat, melt the butter with the oil. Add the lamb and cook, turning often, until browned on all sides, 5–7 minutes. Transfer the lamb to a large covered ovenproof casserole.

Pour off any remaining fat from the skillet, add the beef stock, and increase the heat to high. Bring the stock to a boil, stirring to pick up any browned bits left in the bottom of the skillet. Pour over the lamb in the casserole, cover, and cook in the oven for 1 hour.

Add the carrots, potatoes, turnip, and onion to the casserole. Cook 30 minutes longer, or until the vegetables are soft. Season the stew with salt and pepper. Serve in warmed bowls.

Lamb Shanks with Brown Flour Gravy

SERVES 4

The lamb shanks should be cooked long enough to make them silky-soft-tender. Browned flour is an old-fashioned way to transform pan drippings into a nutty-flavored rich gravy.

FOR THE SHANKS

4 meaty lamb shanks (about ¾ pound each), at room temperature
1 cup flour
1 teaspoon salt
½ teaspoon freshly ground black pepper
2 tablespoons (¼ stick) unsalted butter
2 tablespoons vegetable oil
1 large onion, thinly sliced
1 cup hearty red wine, Beef Stock (page 29), or water

1 bay leaf
Several sprigs fresh thyme

FOR THE GRAVY

2 tablespoons flour
1 cup hearty red wine, Beef Stock (page 29), or water
Salt and freshly ground black pepper to taste
1 tablespoon finely chopped fresh parsley

To cook the shanks, preheat the oven to 350°F. Trim the shanks of excess fat. In a large shallow bowl, mix together the flour, salt, and pepper. Add the shanks and roll to coat on all sides. Shake off any excess flour.

In a large skillet over medium-high heat, melt the butter with the oil. Add the shanks and cook, turning often, until browned on all sides, 5–7 minutes.

Transfer the shanks to a heavy covered ovenproof casserole or Dutch oven.

Pour off all the fat from the skillet and add the onion. Cook over medium heat, stirring constantly, until softened, 3–5 minutes. Pour in the wine, beef stock, or water, increase the heat to high, and bring to a boil, stirring to pick up any browned bits left in the bottom of the skillet. Pour the onion and all the liquid over the shanks. Add the bay leaf and thyme, cover, and cook in the oven until very tender, about 2 hours. Watch carefully. Turn the shanks often and add more wine, stock, or water if needed to prevent scorching.

Discard the bay leaf. Transfer the shanks to a platter and cover with foil to keep warm. Skim off any fat from the pan juices and place the casserole on top of the stove.

To make the gravy, sprinkle the flour over the pan juices in the bottom of the casserole. Whisk over medium-high heat until the flour is lightly browned, about 5 minutes. Pour in the wine, beef stock, or water and stir until the mixture is thickened and simmering, about 5 minutes. Season with salt and pepper.

Strain the gravy over the shanks. Garnish with parsley and serve on warmed plates.

King's Arms Tavern Rack of Lamb

1 young rack of lamb (rib end of the
saddle or double loin with 8 chops,
about 1 pound each), at room
temperature
2 teaspoons salt
1 teaspoon garlic powder

1 teaspoon onion powder
1 teaspoon finely chopped fresh
rosemary
½ teaspoon freshly ground black pepper
1–2 tablespoons Dijon mustard
1 cup fine bread crumbs

Preheat the oven to 450°F. and oil a large roasting pan. Trim the rack of excess fat. In
a small bowl, mix together the salt, garlic powder, onion powder, rosemary, and pepper. Use your fingers to rub this mixture into the lamb.

Spread the mustard thinly over the surface of the fat side of the rack. Gently pat on
the bread crumbs to form an even crust. In the roasting pan, place the rack, fat side up,
and roast for 20–25 minutes, or until a meat thermometer inserted into the thickest
part of the flesh reads 140°F. for medium rare. Remove from the pan and let sit for
5–10 minutes, loosely covered with foil. Cut between the ribs to serve.

Veal Collops with Lemon, Capers, and Cream

SERVES 6

*"Collops" is an old English word for cutlets, thin slices of meat usually
cut from the leg. Because the cutlets are pounded thin, they cook quickly
and can be very tough if cooked too long.*

6 thin veal cutlets (6–8 ounces each)
Salt and freshly ground black pepper to
   taste
¼ cup (½ stick) unsalted butter
1 small shallot, minced
1 teaspoon grated lemon peel
1 tablespoon finely chopped fresh
   parsley

½ cup dry white wine
¼ cup Chicken Stock (page 24) or
   low-salt canned chicken stock
2 tablespoons lemon juice
½ cup heavy cream
2 tablespoons capers, drained and finely
   chopped

Pound the cutlets as thin as possible between layers of waxed paper with a mallet or
heavy rolling pin. Season with salt and pepper. In a large skillet over medium-high
heat, melt the butter. Working in batches, add as many of the cutlets as will lie flat in
the skillet. (Do not overcrowd the skillet or the cutlets will not brown properly.) Cook
until lightly browned, about 1 minute on each side. Transfer to a warmed platter and
cover loosely with foil to keep warm. Continue until all the cutlets have been cooked.

Pour out all but 1 tablespoon of the fat from the skillet. Add the shallot and cook,
stirring often, until softened, 2–3 minutes. Add the lemon peel and parsley. Pour in the
wine and increase the heat to high. Boil, stirring to scrape up any browned bits in the
bottom of the skillet, until reduced by half, 3–5 minutes. Pour in the chicken stock and
lemon juice and bring back to a boil. Boil again until reduced by half, about 3 minutes.
Add the cream and bring back to a boil. Boil again until reduced and thick enough to
coat the back of a spoon, 3–5 minutes. Stir in the capers and season with salt and pepper. Spoon the sauce over the cutlets and serve at once.

Stuffed Veal with Mushrooms and Artichokes

SERVES 6

Thin scallops of turkey breast can also be prepared this way.

6 veal cutlets (6 ounces each)
12 tablespoons (1½ sticks) unsalted
  butter, divided
1 large onion, finely chopped
1½ cups fresh bread crumbs
½ cup raisins
Salt and freshly ground black pepper to
  taste

½ teaspoon finely chopped fresh thyme
¼ cup flour
½ cup dry sherry
1 cup Brown Sauce (page 109)
12 ounces fresh mushrooms, quartered
6 small artichoke bottoms, quartered
2 tablespoons finely chopped fresh
  parsley

Cut the veal cutlets in half and pound each thin between layers of waxed paper with a mallet or heavy rolling pin. In a large heavy saucepan over medium-high heat, melt 4 tablespoons of the butter. Add the onion and cook, stirring often, until softened, about 5 minutes. Stir in the bread crumbs, raisins, salt and pepper, and thyme. Remove from the heat.

Spoon 2 tablespoons of the mixture close to one edge of each flattened piece of veal, roll up, and secure with toothpicks. Season the veal with salt and pepper. Roll lightly in the flour to coat on all sides. In a large skillet over medium-high heat, heat 4 tablespoons of the butter and cook the veal until browned on all sides, 7–10 minutes. Remove to a warmed platter and cover loosely with foil to keep warm. Pour off the fat from the skillet and add the sherry. Stir over high heat for 1–2 minutes, scraping up any browned bits from the bottom. Add the brown sauce and return the veal to the skillet. Reduce the heat to low and simmer, covered, until tender when pierced with a fork, 20–30 minutes.

In a skillet over medium-high heat, cook the mushrooms and artichokes in the remaining 4 tablespoons of butter until tender, about 10 minutes.

Place the veal on a heated platter, pour the sauce over, and garnish with the mushrooms, artichokes, and parsley.

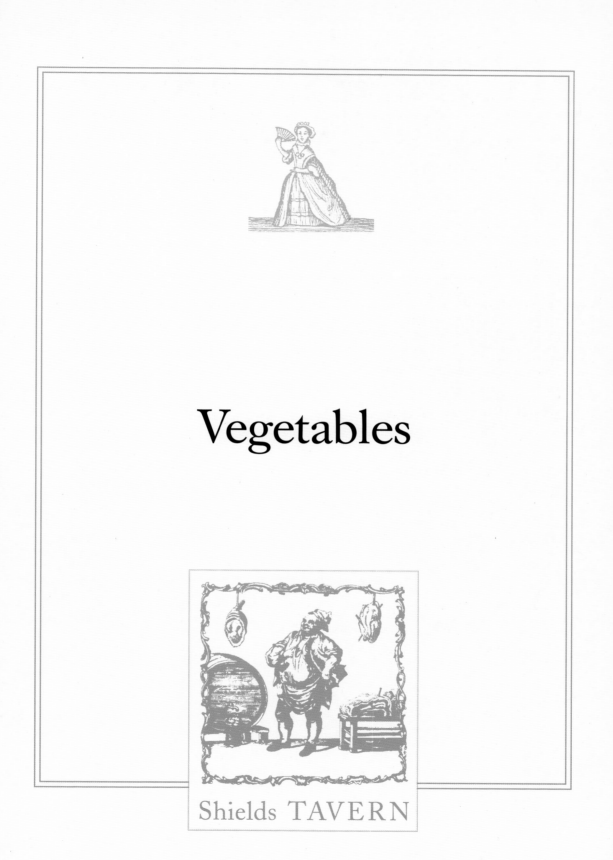

Vegetables

Shields TAVERN

ARTICHOKES, asparagus, beans of all sorts, beets, broccoli, cabbages, carrots, cauliflower, celery, collards, corn, cucumbers, eggplants, kale, leeks, lettuce, onions, parsnips, peas, peppers, potatoes, and turnips—among other vegetables—grew in early Williamsburg gardens. The colonists knew how to prepare and serve them in appetizing ways. In 1745, Hannah Glasse warned: "Most People spoil Garden Things by over boiling them: all things that are Green should have a little Crispness." Mary Randolph's advice about how to prepare asparagus is still valid: "Great care must be taken to watch the exact time of their becoming tender; take them [off] just at that instant, and they will have their true flavour and colour; a minute or two more boiling destroys both."

Like their English counterparts, Virginia housewives took responsibility for planting, cultivating, and harvesting the kitchen garden themselves or overseeing slave gardeners. Since none of their gardening records survives, food historians turn to those gentlemen gardeners—including Thomas Jefferson and Williamsburg residents John Randolph and Joseph Prentis—who had the leisure to record the successes and failures of their gardening pursuits. Randolph's "Treatise on Gardening" is especially useful because it shows how he adapted English methods of growing herbs and vegetables to the warmer, more humid climate of Tidewater Virginia.

By the mid-eighteenth century, tomatoes became popular as a flavoring in soups and sauces in Europe. Williamsburg residents learned about tomatoes about this time too. A notation on the back of a portrait of the town's physician, Dr. John de Sequeyra, states that he "first introduced to Williamsburg the custom of eating tomatoes, until then considered more of a flower than a vegetable."

Hoppin' John

SERVES 8–10

West Africans almost certainly brought the idea for this mixture of rice and black-eyed peas when they came to the New World as slaves. In the South, eating Hoppin' John on New Year's Day is said to bring good luck throughout the year.

8 ounces (2 cups) dried black-eyed peas, soaked overnight and drained
½ pound lean bacon, finely chopped
1 onion, finely chopped
1 celery rib, finely chopped
1 green bell pepper, cored and finely chopped

1 clove garlic, minced
2½ cups long-grain rice, rinsed in cold water
Salt and freshly ground black pepper to taste
¼ teaspoon Tabasco sauce or to taste

Rinse and drain the peas. In a large soup pot or kettle, place the peas and pour in enough cold water to cover by 1 inch, about 6 cups. Bring to a boil over high heat, reduce the heat to medium low, cover, and simmer until the peas are tender, 40–45 minutes.

In a large skillet over medium-high heat, cook the bacon, stirring often, until crisp and the fat is rendered. Remove the bacon with a slotted spoon and drain on paper towels. Pour off all but 2 tablespoons of the fat. Add the onion, celery, and green pepper. Cook over medium heat, stirring often, until softened, 5–7 minutes. Add the garlic and cook 1 minute longer. Stir in the rice and cook, stirring, until translucent, about 5 minutes.

Stir the rice mixture into the peas, cover tightly, and reduce the heat to low. Cook until the rice is dry and fluffy, 20–30 minutes. Fluff the rice with a fork and season with salt and pepper and Tabasco sauce. Add the cooked bacon just before serving.

Port-Braised Red Cabbage

SERVES 6–8

Serve with roast pork or grilled sausages. Add a peeled, cored, and diced apple
or a handful of golden raisins for a festive touch.

1 small red cabbage (1½ pounds)
¼ cup (½ stick) unsalted butter
1 cup Port

Salt and freshly ground black pepper to
 taste
½ cup red wine vinegar

Preheat the oven to 350°F. Remove the tough outer leaves from the head of cabbage. Cut in half and remove the core. Thinly slice the cabbage and rinse under cold running water. Drain well.

In a large covered casserole on top of the stove, melt the butter. Add the Port and the cabbage. Stir well and season with salt and pepper. Cover tightly and place in the oven. Cook, stirring often, until the cabbage is slightly tender, about 20 minutes. Pour in the vinegar, cover, and cook until the cabbage is very soft, about 15 minutes. Watch carefully and add a small amount of water if the cabbage starts to scorch. Season with salt and pepper just before serving.

Carrots Glazed with Two Gingers

SERVES 6

12 medium carrots (2 pounds), peeled
 and sliced
Salt
¼ cup (½ stick) unsalted butter
1 tablespoon honey

1 tablespoon lemon juice
1 tablespoon finely chopped crystallized
 ginger
½ teaspoon ground ginger
Freshly ground black pepper to taste

In a large saucepan, place the carrots and pour in enough cold water to cover. Add salt and bring to a boil over high heat. Reduce the heat to medium and simmer until tender but not mushy, about 10 minutes. Drain and rinse under cold running water. Drain completely on paper towels.

In a large skillet over medium-high heat, melt the butter. Add the honey, lemon juice, crystallized ginger, and ground ginger. Return the carrots to the skillet. Stir gently until the carrots are coated and glazed. Reduce the heat to low, cover, and cook until heated through, 2–3 minutes. Watch carefully and add a small amount of water if the carrots start to scorch. Season with salt and pepper just before serving.

Corn Fritters

SERVES 4

Virginia cooks serve the fritters drizzled with honey.

2 cups fresh or frozen corn kernels
1 small onion, finely chopped
1 tablespoon finely chopped fresh
  parsley
2 large eggs, separated
¼ cup plus 2 tablespoons flour

Salt and freshly ground black pepper to
  taste
¼–½ cup milk
2 tablespoons (¼ stick) unsalted butter
2 tablespoons vegetable oil

In a small bowl, combine the corn, onion, parsley, and egg yolks. Stir in the flour and season with salt and pepper. Add enough milk to form a stiff batter. Beat the egg whites until stiff and fold into the corn mixture.

In a large skillet over medium-high heat, melt the butter with the oil. Drop the batter into the hot oil using a tablespoon and make 4 small fritters at a time. Work in batches to avoid crowding the skillet. Cook until puffed, crisp, and browned, 3–4 minutes per side. Drain on paper towels and serve warm.

Corn Pudding

SERVES 6

*An easy dish to prepare, this corn pudding is baked in a pan of hot water
like a custard. For a light variation, separate the eggs. Add the yolks to the
corn mixture as directed and, in another bowl, beat the whites until stiff peaks form.
Fold the whites into the corn mixture just before pouring into the casserole.
(Use a 2-quart casserole container if you make this version.)*

3 large eggs
2 cups corn kernels, thawed if frozen
1½ tablespoons sugar
½ teaspoon salt
1 cup fresh bread crumbs

2 tablespoons (¼ stick) unsalted butter,
  melted
2 cups milk
½ cup light cream or half-and-half

Preheat the oven to 350°F. and butter a 1½-quart casserole.

In a medium bowl, beat the eggs until light and fluffy. Stir in the corn, sugar, salt, bread crumbs, and melted butter. Add the milk and cream. Pour into the prepared casserole and place in a larger pan of boiling water. Bake until the custard is set and the top is lightly browned, 50–60 minutes.

Collard Greens

SERVES 8–12

*Serve with bottled hot pepper sauce on the side
and plenty of fresh corn bread for sopping up the juices.*

5–6 pounds collard greens, well washed
  and trimmed
6 cups Chicken Stock (page 24),
  low-salt canned chicken stock, or
  water
1 meaty ham hock

1 small dried hot pepper, or ½ teaspoon
  crushed red pepper flakes
2 tablespoons red wine vinegar
½ teaspoon sugar
Salt and freshly ground black pepper to
  taste

Remove the tough bottom stems from the collards and cut the leaves into wide strips. Into a large soup pot or kettle over high heat, pour the chicken stock or water and bring to a boil. Add the greens and the ham hock. Reduce the heat to medium and simmer, stirring often, until the greens are wilted, about 15 minutes. Add the hot pepper and vinegar. Cook until the greens are very tender and the broth is full flavored, about 1 hour. Season with the sugar and salt and pepper just before serving.

Shields Tavern Carrot Pudding Spiced with Cardamom

SERVES 10–12

Pan-roast whole cardamom pods, cool, and reduce to a powder in a spice grinder to increase the flavor of this exotic spice.

3 large eggs, separated
2 tablespoons sugar
1½ tablespoons cornstarch
1 cup milk
2 pounds medium carrots (about
  3 cups), peeled, cooked, and mashed

3 tablespoons unsalted butter
1 teaspoon salt
1 cup fresh bread crumbs
1 cup light cream or half-and-half
½ teaspoon ground cardamom

Preheat the oven to 300°F. and butter a 2-quart casserole. In a small bowl, beat the egg yolks with the sugar until light and fluffy.

Mix the cornstarch with a small amount of the milk. Heat the remaining milk over low heat. Add the cornstarch and stir until the mixture is smooth and slightly thickened.

Stir a small amount of the hot cornstarch mixture into the egg yolks and sugar. Stir well and pour the yolk mixture into the hot milk and cornstarch. Cook over medium-low heat, stirring constantly, until smooth and thick, about 5 minutes. Stir in the carrots, butter, salt, and bread crumbs. Add the cream and cardamom.

Beat the egg whites until they hold firm peaks and fold into the carrot mixture. Pour into the casserole. Place the casserole in a larger pan of hot water and bake for 30 minutes. Increase the heat to 350°F. and bake for an additional 45 minutes, or until a knife inserted in the center comes out clean.

Christiana Campbell's Tavern Bean and Corn Succotash

SERVES 6

"Succotash" comes from "Misickquatosh," a Native American name for a dish of corn and kidney beans cooked in bear grease. Today's version–minus the bear grease–also contains onion, green pepper, hominy, lima beans, peas, black beans, and chickpeas.

2 cups fresh or frozen corn kernels
¼ cup (½ stick) unsalted butter
1 small onion, finely chopped
½ green bell pepper, cut into tiny dice
2 cups canned hominy, drained
½ cup fresh or frozen baby lima
  beans

½ cup fresh or frozen field peas or lady
  peas
½ cup canned black beans, rinsed
½ cup canned kidney beans, rinsed
½ cup canned chickpeas, rinsed
Salt and freshly ground black pepper to
  taste

Place the corn in a medium saucepan. Add 1 tablespoon water and cook over medium heat until tender, about 5 minutes. Drain well.

In a large saucepan over medium-high heat, melt the butter. Add the onion and pepper. Cook, stirring often, until softened, about 5 minutes. Stir in the hominy and cook 5 minutes longer. Add the lima beans, peas, black beans, kidney beans, and chickpeas. Season with salt and pepper, cover, and heat over medium-low heat for about 5 minutes.

Grits Soufflé

SERVES 6

A grits soufflé usually rises and then falls. It resembles spoon bread more than it does a cheese soufflé. For a tasty variation, add ½ cup grated cheese and a dash of Tabasco sauce just before folding in the egg whites.

2 cups milk
½ cup instant grits
1 teaspoon salt
½ teaspoon baking powder
2 tablespoons (¼ stick) unsalted butter, melted

½ teaspoon sugar
3 large eggs, separated
½ cup grated Cheddar cheese, if desired
Dash Tabasco sauce, if desired

Preheat the oven to 375° F. and butter a 1½-quart casserole.

In a small saucepan, heat the milk until bubbles form around the edges. Add the grits and cook, stirring constantly, until thickened, 5–7 minutes. Stir in the salt, baking powder, melted butter, and sugar. Beat in the egg yolks one at a time. Add the Cheddar cheese and Tabasco sauce if desired.

Beat the egg whites until they form stiff peaks. Fold into the grits and pour into the casserole. Bake until lightly browned and puffed, about 30 minutes. Serve hot.

Chowning's Tavern Creamy Grits

SERVES 4-6

Salt
1 cup white hominy grits (not quick-cooking grits)

1 tablespoon unsalted butter, softened
½ cup milk or more as needed
Freshly ground black pepper to taste

Into a large saucepan, pour 4 cups of water and add 1 teaspoon salt. Bring to a boil over high heat. Slowly add the grits, stirring constantly, until smooth. Reduce the heat to low and cook, tightly covered, until the grits are softened and the mixture is thickened, about 30 minutes. Stir in the butter and milk, season with salt and pepper, and serve in warmed bowls.

Mashed Caramelized Sweet Potatoes

SERVES 8–10

3 pounds sweet potatoes
¾ cup packed light brown sugar, divided
3 tablespoons unsalted butter
½ teaspoon ground cinnamon

½ teaspoon grated nutmeg
¼ teaspoon salt
1 cup milk
Freshly ground black pepper to taste

In a large pot, place the sweet potatoes and pour in enough cold water to cover. Add a pinch of salt and bring to a boil over high heat. Reduce the heat to medium and cook until tender, about 45 minutes. Cool, peel, and mash the cooked sweet potatoes.

Preheat the oven to 400°F. and butter a 2-quart casserole.

Reserve 2 tablespoons of the sugar for the topping. In a large bowl, combine the remaining sugar, butter, cinnamon, nutmeg, ¼ teaspoon salt, and milk. Stir in the mashed sweet potatoes and season with additional salt and pepper. Transfer to the casserole and sprinkle the remaining sugar over. Bake until the potatoes are hot and the sugar has melted and slightly caramelized, about 20–30 minutes.

Sweet Potatoes or Yams?

ARE SWEET POTATOES AND YAMS THE SAME? NO. NATIVE TO SOUTH AMERICA, THE SWEET POTATO GROWS WELL IN TIDEWATER VIRGINIA. THE YAM, A TROPICAL PLANT NATIVE TO AFRICA, DOESN'T GROW IN THE CONTINENTAL UNITED STATES. MOST OF THE VARIETIES WITH DARKER FLESH DESIGNATED AS "YAMS" ARE ACTUALLY SWEET POTATOES. IMPORTED TRUE YAMS CAN SOMETIMES BE FOUND IN LATIN MARKETS.

Green Beans Baked with Smoked Ham Hock

SERVES 4–6

These wide, mature beans must cook for a long time with a bit of pork for flavor.

2 pounds wide, mature green beans or
   pole beans
1 meaty smoked ham hock

1 medium onion, thinly sliced
Salt and freshly ground black pepper to
   taste

Preheat the oven to 350°F.

Remove the tough strings along the sides of the beans. Cut the beans into 1-inch pieces. In a small covered casserole, place the beans and add the ham hock. Sprinkle the onion over and season with salt and pepper. Pour in just enough water to cover the beans. Cover and bake until the beans are tender, about 1 hour. Stir often, adding more water if necessary to prevent the beans from scorching. Cut the lean part of the hock into small pieces and serve with the beans if desired.

Creamed Spinach

1½ pounds cooked or thawed frozen
  spinach, squeezed dry
2 tablespoons (¼ stick) unsalted butter
2 tablespoons flour

1 cup milk
¼ teaspoon grated nutmeg
⅛ teaspoon cayenne pepper
Salt and freshly ground black pepper

Finely chop the spinach and set aside.

In a small saucepan over medium-high heat, melt the butter. Add the flour and stir until well blended and lemon colored, about 3 minutes. Pour in the milk, increase the heat to high, and bring to a boil. Reduce the heat to medium and season with the nutmeg, cayenne, and salt and pepper.

Add the chopped spinach to the sauce and stir occasionally until heated through, about 5 minutes. Season again with salt and pepper just before serving.

King's Arms Tavern Creamed Onions with Peanuts

16 whole small white onions, peeled
2 tablespoons (¼ stick) unsalted butter
2 tablespoons flour
2 cups milk

¼ cup whole salted peanuts
½ cup buttered fresh bread crumbs
¼ cup coarsely chopped salted peanuts

Preheat the oven to 400°F. and butter a 1-quart casserole. Cook the onions in boiling salted water until tender and drain.

In a small saucepan over medium-high heat, melt the butter. Add the flour and stir until well blended and lemon colored, about 3 minutes. Pour in the milk, increase the heat to high, and bring to a boil, stirring often. Reduce the heat to medium and cook until smooth and thickened, 5–7 minutes.

Put the onions in the casserole and pour the sauce over. Stir in the whole peanuts and top with the buttered crumbs. Sprinkle the chopped peanuts over and bake until lightly browned on top and bubbly, about 15 minutes.

Christiana Campbell's Tavern Saffron Rice Pilaf

SERVES 4–6

1 cup long-grain rice
2 tablespoons (¼ stick) unsalted butter
Salt

½ teaspoon powdered saffron
Freshly ground black pepper

In a colander under cold running water, rinse the rice and transfer to a medium heavy saucepan with a tight-fitting lid. Pour in 2½ cups cold water and bring to a boil over high heat. Reduce the heat to medium low, cover, and cook for 20 minutes. Remove the lid, fluff the rice with a fork, and add the butter, 1 teaspoon salt, and the saffron. Cover and let sit for 5 minutes. Season with salt and pepper before serving.

King's Arms Tavern Stewed Tomatoes and Eggplant

SERVES 4

Toss the cubes of eggplant with salt and set aside for 30 minutes before cooking to draw out the bitter juices. Rinse under cold running water and pat dry before cooking.

2 tablespoons (¼ stick) unsalted butter
1 large onion, thinly sliced
1 medium eggplant, peeled and cut into
   1-inch cubes

6 medium ripe tomatoes, peeled, seeded,
   and chopped
1 teaspoon chopped fresh thyme
Salt and freshly ground black pepper to
   taste

In a heavy nonreactive saucepan with a tight-fitting lid over medium-high heat, melt the butter. Add the onion and cook, stirring often, until softened, about 5 minutes. Stir in the eggplant and tomatoes. Add the thyme and season well with salt and pepper. Reduce the heat to medium low and cover. Cook, stirring often, until the eggplant is very soft and the tomatoes have given off most of their juices, about 1 hour.

    If the stew appears too watery, remove the cover and increase the heat to high. Boil rapidly until thick and pulpy. Season again with salt and pepper just before serving.

Martha Washington's Mushrooms in Cream Sauce

SERVES 4

Creamed "mushrumps," an old English term for mushrooms, are served in a hollowed-out bread roll at Shields Tavern.

12 ounces fresh mushrooms, trimmed
2 tablespoons (¼ stick) unsalted
   butter
1 cup heavy cream

1 tablespoon finely chopped fresh
   parsley
Salt and freshly ground white pepper to
   taste

Halve or quarter the mushrooms. (They should be uniformly cut to cook evenly.) In a large skillet over medium-high heat, melt the butter. Add the mushrooms and cook, stirring and shaking the pan often, until lightly browned and softened, about 5 minutes. Pour in the cream, increase the heat to high, and boil rapidly until slightly thickened, 3–5 minutes. Stir in the parsley, season with salt and pepper, and serve very hot.

Breads

NATIVE Americans introduced the first English settlers to corn bread in the form of ashcakes, a mixture of cornmeal and water shaped into little flat cakes that were baked in the ashes. A century later, historian Robert Beverley wrote that "the Bread in Gentlemen's Houses, is generally made of Wheat, but some rather choose the Pone, which is the Bread made of *Indian Meal* . . . from the Indian Name *Oppone.*"

Slaves and the poorer sort continued to eat pone, which they called hoe-cakes when the little cakes were baked atop a hoe blade on the hearth or by field hands over an open fire. If corn bread was served in gentry houses such as Mount Vernon—"Indian cakes for breakfast after the Virginia fashion"—cooks enriched it with butter, eggs, milk, and yeast.

Slaves did most of the baking and cooking in the kitchens of gentry homes. Busy cooks baked quick breads like muffins and biscuits in an iron Dutch oven in the coals of the fireplace. Affluent Virginians also enjoyed yeast rolls made from wheat flour.

PREVIOUS PAGES, CLOCKWISE FROM TOP RIGHT: Martha Washington's Potato Rolls, Blueberry-Orange Loaf, assorted muffins, and Sally Lunn.

King's Arms Tavern Apple Cheddar Muffins

MAKES 16 MUFFINS

2 cups flour
1 tablespoon baking powder
¼ teaspoon baking soda
½ teaspoon cinnamon
½ teaspoon salt
¼ cup (½ stick) unsalted butter, softened
¼ cup sugar

2 large eggs
1 cup sour cream
2 medium apples, such as Golden Delicious, peeled, cored, and finely chopped
½ cup grated Cheddar cheese

Preheat the oven to 425°F. and butter 16 muffin cups, each 2½ inches in diameter.

In a large bowl, mix together the flour, baking powder, baking soda, cinnamon, and salt.

In a separate large bowl, cream the butter with the sugar until light and fluffy. Beat in the eggs one at a time. Stir in the sour cream.

Add the wet ingredients to the dry ingredients all at once and stir to blend. Do not overwork the batter or the muffins will be tough. Stir in the apples and cheese.

Spoon the batter into the muffin cups, filling each about halfway. Bake for 15–20 minutes, or until a toothpick inserted into the center comes out clean. Turn the muffins out of the tins and serve at once.

Mrs. Booth's Biscuit Mix

MAKES 4 ½ CUPS

Letha Booth was the first cook and operator of the earliest restored tavern in Williamsburg. Her biscuits were legendary even if her recipes were a little vague–"add milk as needed," for example. Biscuit makers know that the amount of liquid needed depends on the dryness of the flour and the weather. We suggest a range of 3–4 tablespoons milk per cup of dry mixture.

3 cups self-rising flour, plus more for kneading
1½ teaspoons baking powder
1 tablespoon sugar
1½ teaspoons salt

1 cup chilled vegetable shortening
Milk as needed, 3–4 tablespoons per cup of mix
Melted unsalted butter or additional milk for glazing

In a large bowl, combine the flour, baking powder, sugar, and salt. Add the shortening and with your fingertips, 2 knives, or a pastry blender, cut in the dry ingredients until the mixture resembles the texture of coarse meal.

Preheat the oven to 450°F. For six 2-inch biscuits, combine 1 cup of the mix with just enough milk to moisten, 3–4 tablespoons per cup of mix. Knead lightly on a floured work surface 5–6 times. Roll out the dough ½-inch thick for high biscuits, ¼-inch thick for thin, crusty biscuits. Cut with a biscuit cutter and arrange on a greased cookie sheet. Brush the tops with melted butter or milk. Space the dough close together for soft biscuits, 1 inch apart for crusty ones.

Bake for 7–10 minutes, or until golden brown.

Shields Tavern Indian Corn Muffins

To make corn sticks, increase the milk to 1½ cups. Grease 14–16 corn stick molds, heat the molds until hot, pour in the batter, and bake for about 12–15 minutes or until browned on top and a toothpick inserted in the center comes out clean.

1 cup cornmeal
1 cup flour
2½ teaspoons baking powder
1 teaspoon salt

2 large eggs, lightly beaten
1 cup milk
2 tablespoons melted vegetable
  shortening

Preheat the oven to 400°F. and butter 12 muffin cups, each 2½ inches in diameter.

In a large bowl, stir the cornmeal, flour, baking powder, and salt. In a small bowl, beat the eggs and milk until well blended. Stir into the dry ingredients just until mixed. Blend in the melted shortening.

Pour the batter into the muffin cups and bake for about 20 minutes, or until lightly browned on top and a toothpick inserted into the center comes out clean. Turn out onto wire racks. Serve warm.

Corn Bread

SERVES 8–10

1 cup cornmeal
1 cup flour
2 teaspoons baking powder
½ teaspoon baking soda

1 teaspoon salt
1 large egg, lightly beaten
1 cup buttermilk
¼ cup melted vegetable shortening

Preheat the oven to 400°F. and lightly grease an 8- or 9-inch pan.

In a large bowl, stir the cornmeal, flour, baking powder, baking soda, and salt. In a small bowl, beat the egg and the buttermilk until well blended. Stir into the dry ingredients just until mixed. Blend in the melted shortening.

Pour the batter into the baking pan and bake for 20–25 minutes, or until lightly browned on top and a toothpick inserted into the center comes out clean. Turn out onto a wire rack and cool. Cut into squares and serve.

Blueberry-Orange Loaf

MAKES 1 LOAF

2 cups flour
1 cup plus ½ tablespoon sugar
1½ teaspoons baking powder
½ teaspoon baking soda
½ teaspoon salt

¼ cup (½ stick) unsalted butter, chilled,
   cut into small pieces
1 large egg, lightly beaten
1 tablespoon finely grated orange peel
½ cup orange juice
1½ cups fresh blueberries

Preheat the oven to 350°F. and butter a 9 × 5-inch loaf pan.

In a large bowl, stir together the flour, sugar, baking powder, baking soda, and salt. Add the butter and with your fingertips, 2 knives, or a pastry blender, cut in the dry ingredients until the texture resembles coarse meal.

In a small bowl, beat together the egg, orange peel, and orange juice. Add to the flour mixture and stir to blend. Stir in the blueberries. Stir just until the ingredients are thoroughly combined.

Spoon the batter into the prepared pan and smooth the top with a spatula. Sprinkle with the remaining ½ tablespoon sugar. Bake for about 50 minutes or until a toothpick inserted into the center comes out clean. Cool on a wire rack before slicing.

Johnnycakes

SERVES 4–6

Travelers sometimes made dense, sturdy cakes like these to take on trips.
Some say the word "johnny" is a derivation of "journey."

1 cup cornmeal
½ teaspoon salt
1½ cups boiling water

2 tablespoons (¼ stick) unsalted butter
1½ cups buttermilk

In a large heavy saucepan, combine the cornmeal and salt. Pour in the boiling water, whisking constantly, and cook over medium-high heat until thick, about 10 minutes. Remove from the heat and stir in the butter and buttermilk.

Drop heaping tablespoons of batter onto a lightly greased griddle over medium heat. Cook until the undersides are golden brown, about 5 minutes. Turn and cook on the other sides until lightly browned, about 5 minutes. Serve warm.

Martha Washington's Potato Rolls

MAKES 24 ROLLS

2 medium all-purpose potatoes, peeled
  and cut into 1-inch cubes
1 (2¼-teaspoons) package active dry
  yeast
½ cup plus 1 teaspoon sugar
5–6 cups flour

½ teaspoon salt
2 large eggs
½ cup (1 stick) unsalted butter, softened
1 large egg yolk beaten with
  1 tablespoon milk

In a medium saucepan, place the potatoes and pour in enough cold water to cover. Bring to a boil over high heat, reduce the heat to medium, and cook until tender, 10–15 minutes. Drain, reserving 1 cup of the potato water. Mash the potatoes in a ricer or food mill and measure. You should have 1 cup pureed potatoes.

Cool the potato cooking water to lukewarm, about 110°F. In a small bowl, combine ¼ cup of the water with the yeast and 1 teaspoon sugar. Stir well and set aside until bubbles form around the edges of the bowl, about 5 minutes.

In the bowl of a standing electric mixer fitted with a dough hook, mix 5 cups of the flour, ½ cup sugar, and the salt. Add the pureed potatoes, remaining ¾ cup potato water, eggs, and butter. Beat on low speed for about 1 minute. Add additional flour in ¼-cup increments as needed to make a stiff dough. The dough should easily pull away from the sides of the bowl. Increase the speed to medium and knead until the dough is very smooth and elastic, about 10 minutes. Transfer to a large buttered bowl and cover with plastic wrap. Place in a warm, draft-free spot (75°–85°F.) and let rise until doubled in bulk, 1–2 hours.

Generously butter 24 muffin cups, each 2½ inches in diameter. Turn the dough out onto a lightly floured work surface. Gently punch down the dough and quickly knead into a smooth ball. Pinch off small pieces and roll into 1-inch balls. Place 3 balls in each muffin cup. Cover with a cloth and set aside to rise until the balls have almost doubled in bulk, about 30 minutes.

Preheat the oven to 425°F. Brush the rolls with the egg yolk and milk mixture. Bake for 15–18 minutes, or until browned.

Sally Lunn

SERVES 16–24

Sally Lunn, named for a young woman who sold her breads on the streets in eighteenth-century Bath, England, was very popular in the colonial South. The story goes that a "respectable baker and musician" bought Sally's business and wrote a song about her. The crumbly bread has become a Virginia favorite. Serve warm with softened butter.

1 cup milk
½ cup vegetable shortening
4 cups flour, divided
⅓ cup sugar

2 teaspoons salt
2 (2¼-teaspoon) packages active dry yeast
3 large eggs

In a small saucepan, combine the milk, shortening, and ¼ cup water. Warm over medium-low heat until a thermometer reaches 120°F. (The shortening does not need to melt.)

In a large bowl, blend 1⅓ cups of the flour with the sugar, salt, and yeast. Blend the warm liquids into the flour mixture. Beat with an electric mixer at medium speed for 2 minutes. Add the remaining flour and the eggs. Mix well. The batter will be thick but not stiff. Cover and let the dough rise in a warm, draft-free spot (75°–85°F.) until doubled in bulk, about 1¼ hours.

Grease a 10-inch tube pan or Bundt pan. Beat the dough down with a spatula or electric mixer set on low speed. Turn into the prepared pan, cover, and let rise in a warm spot until almost doubled in bulk, about 30 minutes.

Preheat the oven to 350°F. Bake for 40–50 minutes, or until golden brown. Run a knife around the center and outer edges of the bread. Turn out onto a wire rack to cool.

Sippets

6 SERVINGS

Sippet is the diminutive form of the Old English word "sop," to soak up, as in gravy or sauce. These strips of toast can be made with good-quality challah or brioche if Sally Lunn is not available. Butter lightly before toasting for added color and flavor.

6 ½-inch-thick slices Sally Lunn bread (page 163) or other firm white bread

Unsalted butter (optional)

Trim the crusts from the bread. Cut each slice into 4 horizontal strips. Butter lightly, if desired. Brown the sippets in a preheated 375°F. oven or toast lightly.

Spoon Bread

SERVES 8

Spoon bread is a soufflé-like custard cornbread that is served as true bread or as a side dish in place of rice or potatoes. Spooned directly from the dish it was baked in, this Virginia classic is now enjoyed throughout the country. For a lighter version, separate the eggs. Add the yolks to the baking powder as directed and beat the whites until stiff. Gently fold the whites into the batter just before pouring into the baking dish.

2 cups milk
1 ½ cups cornmeal
1 ½ teaspoons sugar
1 ¼ teaspoons salt

2 tablespoons (¼ stick) unsalted butter
5 large eggs
1 tablespoon baking powder

Preheat the oven to 350°F. and butter a 2-quart baking dish.

In a large heavy saucepan over medium heat, combine 1 ½ cups water and the milk. Bring to a simmer and add the cornmeal, sugar, salt, and butter. Stir until the mixture is thickened, about 5 minutes. Remove from the heat and cool slightly.

In a medium bowl, beat the eggs with the baking powder until light and fluffy. Stir into the cornmeal mixture.

Pour the batter into the baking dish and bake for 45–50 minutes, or until lightly browned on top and puffy. Serve hot.

Christiana Campbell's Tavern Sweet Potato Muffins

1 cup flour

1 teaspoon baking powder

½ teaspoon salt

1 teaspoon cinnamon

½ teaspoon grated nutmeg

¼ cup (½ stick) unsalted butter, softened

½ cup sugar

2 large eggs

1 cup mashed cooked sweet potatoes

½ cup milk

½ cup chopped pecans or walnuts

½ cup raisins

Preheat the oven to 400°F. and butter 24 mini-muffin cups, each 1¾ inches wide × 1 inch deep.

Into a large bowl, sift the flour with the baking powder, salt, cinnamon, and nutmeg.

In a separate bowl, beat the butter with the sugar until light and fluffy. Beat in the eggs, sweet potatoes, and milk. Add the wet ingredients to the dry ingredients and mix just until blended. Stir in the nuts and raisins. Fill the muffin cups two thirds full and bake for about 20 minutes, or until a toothpick inserted into the center comes out clean. Turn out onto wire racks and serve at once.

Cakes

and

Cookies

I N the days before baking powder, packaged yeast, and eggbeaters, baking a cake was an arduous task usually reserved for festive occasions. Sugar came in a hard loaf or cone and had to be chipped and then pounded into powder. Flour was sifted at least once just to remove bugs and coarse hulls of grain. Spices were crushed, grated, or pulverized; raisins and currants were seeded. Then the mixture was beaten by hand–literally–for an hour or more. Cooks learned from experience how to regulate the temperature in a colonial oven.

Despite these obstacles, Virginia housewives filled cookbooks with an incredible variety of cake recipes to serve at balls, weddings, holidays, and even funerals. Perhaps the "black cake that will last a year" if properly stored was a forerunner of today's ubiquitous Christmas fruitcake.

The colonial counterparts of what Americans call "cookies" today were described as "little cakes" or "biscuits" in English cookbooks of the period. Street vendors hawked Shrewsbury sugar cookies spiced with cinnamon and ginger cakes to passersby. Thomas Jefferson "paid at Capitol for cakes 7 1/2 d" in 1771. Fancier small cakes–jumbals, macaroons, and ratafia cakes–appeared on dessert tables.

"Cookie" is a corruption of *koekje,* the Dutch word for a small cake. In the eighteenth century, New Yorkers borrowed the term from their Dutch neighbors and it caught on. Amelia Simmons gave recipes for "Cookies" and "Christmas cookey" in *American Cookery* (1796). Instead of baking powder, both recipes called for one teaspoon of pearl ash dissolved in milk as the leavening agent.

PREVIOUS PAGES: Right, *King's Arms Tavern Seven-Layer Chocolate Torte.*
Left, top tier: *Bourbon Balls.* Middle tier, left to right: *Shields Tavern Gingersnaps,*
Pecan Bars, King's Arms Tavern Macaroons. Bottom tier, left to right: *Gingerbread,*
Chowning's Tavern Brownies, and Date Nut Pound Cake.

King's Arms Tavern Seven-Layer Chocolate Torte

SERVES 10–12

FOR THE CAKE
1 cup (2 sticks) unsalted butter, softened
1 cup sugar
6 large eggs
2 cups cake flour
2 teaspoons baking powder
1 teaspoon vanilla

FOR THE CHOCOLATE FROSTING
8 ounces unsweetened chocolate, finely
  chopped
1 cup (2 sticks) unsalted butter
6 cups confectioners' sugar
Dash salt
2 teaspoons vanilla
1–1½ cups evaporated milk

To bake the cakes, have all ingredients at room temperature. Preheat the oven to 325°F. and butter two 8-inch round cake pans.

In a large bowl, beat the butter with the sugar until light and fluffy. Add the eggs one at a time, beating well after each addition.

Sift the flour with the baking powder. Gradually beat into the egg mixture. Stir in the vanilla.

Divide the batter between the two pans, placing ½ cup more batter in one pan. Bake the cakes until a toothpick inserted in the centers comes out clean, 25–30 minutes. Let the cakes stand for 10 minutes before turning out to cool completely on wire racks.

Chill the cakes in the freezer for 30 minutes before slicing. With a long serrated knife, carefully cut the larger cake into 4 horizontal layers and the smaller cake into 3 horizontal layers.

To prepare the frosting, in the top of a double boiler over simmering, not boiling, water, melt the chocolate with the butter.

Into a large bowl, sift the sugar with the salt. Stir in the vanilla and the chocolate mixture. Add enough evaporated milk to make the frosting soft enough to spread.

Carefully spread a small amount of the frosting between each of the layers. Stack the layers and frost the outside of the cake with the frosting, using a knife dipped in hot water for spreading and smoothing.

Bourbon Pecan Cake

SERVES 8–10

2 teaspoons grated nutmeg
½ cup bourbon
1½ cups flour, divided
2 cups finely chopped pecans
1 cup finely chopped raisins
½ cup (1 stick) unsalted butter, softened
1 cup plus 2 tablespoons sugar

3 large eggs, separated
1½ teaspoons baking powder
⅛ teaspoon salt
½ cup apple jelly
Pecan halves, for garnish
Candied cherries, for garnish

Preheat the oven to 325°F., butter a 10-inch tube pan, and line the bottom with parchment or waxed paper. Butter the paper and set aside.

In a small bowl, mix the nutmeg with the bourbon and set aside.

In a large bowl, sprinkle ½ cup of the flour over the nuts and raisins. Toss or stir to coat thoroughly.

In a large bowl, beat the butter with the sugar until light and fluffy. Slowly add the nutmeg and bourbon mixture and beat until light and fluffy. Add the egg yolks, one at a time, beating well after each addition. Add the remaining flour, baking powder, and salt. Stir to form a stiff batter. Blend in the floured pecans and raisins. Beat the egg whites until very stiff and fold into the batter.

Spoon the batter into the prepared pan and bake until a toothpick inserted into the center of the cake comes out clean, 1–1¼ hours. Cool in the pan for 1–2 hours before turning out onto a wire rack to cool completely.

In a small saucepan, melt the apple jelly. Brush the top of the cake with the warm jelly and decorate with pecan halves and candied cherries. Brush again to glaze.

Chowning's Tavern Apple Cider Cake

SERVES 10–12

*Use flavorful cooking apples like Rome Beauty, Crispin, Granny Smith,
or Golden Delicious for best results.*

4 medium apples, peeled, cored, and
  finely chopped
2 cups sugar
2 large eggs, lightly beaten
1 cup (2 sticks) butter, melted and
  cooled
3 cups flour

2 teaspoons baking soda
2 teaspoons cinnamon
½ teaspoon grated nutmeg
½ teaspoon allspice
1 cup finely chopped walnuts
1 cup apple cider
½ cup confectioners' sugar

Preheat the oven to 350°F. and butter a 12-cup nonstick Bundt pan. In a large bowl, place the apples and sprinkle over the sugar. Stir well and set aside for 15 minutes, stirring often.

In a large bowl, combine the eggs and butter and mix well. In another large bowl, combine the flour, baking soda, cinnamon, nutmeg, allspice, and walnuts. Add the butter-egg mixture and the reserved apples, and stir well. Pour the batter into the pan, smooth the top with a spatula, and bake until a toothpick inserted in the center comes out clean, about 45 minutes. Let the cake stand in the pan for 10 minutes. Invert onto a wire rack.

In a small saucepan, place the cider and bring to a boil over high heat. Boil until reduced by half. Cool slightly and stir in the confectioners' sugar. Drizzle over the cake while warm. Let the cake cool completely before slicing.

Date Nut Pound Cake

SERVES 8–10

1 cup (2 sticks) unsalted butter, softened
1 cup sugar
6 large eggs
2 cups plus 2 tablespoons flour

½ teaspoon baking powder
1 teaspoon vanilla
½ cup chopped pecans or walnuts
⅓ cup finely chopped pitted dates

Preheat the oven to 325°F. and butter a 9 × 5 × 3-inch loaf pan or a 9-inch tube pan. Dust the pan with flour and shake out the excess.

In a large bowl, beat the butter with the sugar until light and fluffy. Add the eggs one at a time, beating well after each addition.

Sift the 2 cups flour and the baking powder together and gradually stir into the egg mixture. Stir in the vanilla.

In a large bowl, sprinkle the remaining 2 tablespoons flour over the nuts and dates. Toss or stir to coat thoroughly. Fold into the batter.

Spoon the batter into the prepared pan. Bake until a toothpick inserted into the center comes out clean, about 1 hour 10 minutes for the loaf pan or 1 hour for the tube pan. Cool in the pan for 10 minutes. Turn out onto a wire rack and cool completely.

Gingerbread

SERVES 8

Dust with confectioners' sugar after cooling.
Serve with whipped cream flavored with grated lemon peel.

½ cup (1 stick) unsalted butter, softened
¾ cup milk
1 cup packed dark brown sugar
1½ cups flour
1 teaspoon baking soda

¼ teaspoon baking powder
1 tablespoon ground ginger
1 teaspoon cinnamon
⅛ teaspoon salt
1 large egg, lightly beaten

Preheat the oven to 350°F. Butter an 8 × 8 × 2-inch cake pan and line the bottom with parchment or waxed paper. Butter the paper and set aside.

In a small saucepan, combine the butter and milk. Heat over medium-high heat until the butter is melted and bubbles form around the edges of the pan. Whisk in the brown sugar until dissolved. Remove from the heat and cool.

Into a large bowl, sift the flour with the baking soda, baking powder, ginger, cinnamon, and salt.

Stir the egg into the cooled milk mixture. Make a well in the center of the dry ingredients and pour in the liquid. Stir just until the mixture forms a smooth batter. Pour into the pan and bake until a toothpick inserted in the center comes out clean, 25–30 minutes. Turn out onto a wire rack and cool completely before serving.

Bourbon Balls

MAKES 60 SMALL BALLS

Packed in an attractive tin, an offering of these confections is a wonderful holiday gift.

8 ounces semisweet chocolate, finely
  chopped
60 vanilla wafers
1 cup finely chopped pecans

1½ cups sugar
½ cup bourbon
¼ cup light corn syrup

In the top of a double boiler over simmering, not boiling, water, melt the chocolate. Remove from the heat and cool to lukewarm.

In the bowl of a food processor, place the vanilla wafers and process until the cookies are very finely ground. Add the pecans and half the sugar to the processor bowl and process in several quick pulses to blend. Into a large bowl, pour the mixture. Add the cooled chocolate, bourbon, and corn syrup. Stir to mix the ingredients thoroughly.

Working with 1 tablespoon of the dough at a time, roll the cookies into 1-inch balls. Refrigerate for 30 minutes to 1 hour, or until well chilled.

In a large shallow bowl, place the remaining sugar. Roll the balls in the sugar until well coated. Place in a metal container with a tight-fitting lid for at least 12 hours before serving. The cookies will keep for 4–5 weeks.

Chowning's Tavern Brownies

MAKES 20 PIECES

Use imported, top-quality chocolate to make these chewy brownies. Serve with vanilla ice cream and raspberry or chocolate sauce for a special treat.

1 cup (2 sticks) unsalted butter
8 ounces unsweetened chocolate, finely
  chopped
7 large eggs
3 cups sugar

½ teaspoon vanilla
2 cups flour
1 tablespoon baking powder
1 cup coarsely chopped pecans

Preheat the oven to 350°F. and butter a 10 × 15 × 1-inch jellyroll pan.

In the top of a double boiler over simmering, not boiling, water, melt the butter and chocolate.

In a large bowl, beat the eggs, sugar, and vanilla until frothy. Blend in the melted butter and chocolate. Stir in the flour and baking powder. Mix well to form a dark, smooth batter. Stir in the pecans.

Pour the batter into the pan and bake until a toothpick inserted in the center comes out clean, about 30 minutes. Cool and cut into 3 × 3-inch squares.

Shields Tavern Gingersnaps

MAKES 20–30 SMALL COOKIES

¼ cup (½ stick) unsalted butter, softened
¼ cup sugar
1 large egg
¼ cup molasses

1 teaspoon ground ginger
¼ teaspoon baking soda
⅛ teaspoon salt
1½ cups flour

In a large bowl, beat the butter and sugar until light and fluffy. Add the egg and molasses. Stir in the ginger, baking soda, salt, and flour and mix until well combined. Turn out onto a floured work surface and gently knead into a smooth ball. Place the dough in a bowl and cover with plastic wrap. Chill for at least 2 hours or overnight.

Preheat the oven to 350°F. and butter 2 baking sheets. Working with half the dough at a time, roll out to a thickness of ¼ inch. Cut into desired shapes. Transfer to the cookie sheets and bake until lightly browned around the edges and firm in the center, 15–20 minutes. Transfer to wire racks and cool completely before serving.

King's Arms Tavern Almond Macaroons

MAKES 45 SMALL MACAROONS

Almond paste can be found in many specialty food stores.

1 (8-ounce) can almond paste
¾ cup sugar
Pinch of salt

3 large egg whites
½ teaspoon almond extract

Preheat the oven to 350°F. and line 1 or 2 cookie sheets with parchment paper. Break up the almond paste and place in the bowl of an electric mixer. Beat in the sugar and salt. Gradually add the egg whites and almond extract and beat until smooth.

Drop the batter by teaspoonfuls onto the cookie sheets about 2 inches apart. Smooth the tops with a pastry brush moistened with water. Bake until golden and puffed, 15–20 minutes. To remove the cookies, cool slightly, moisten the back of the paper, and peel off.

> IN ADDITION TO APPEARING ON DESSERT TABLES, THE DELICIOUS LITTLE ALMOND-FLAVORED COOKIES CALLED "MACAROONS" WERE BEING SERVED WITH WINE OR LIQUEURS AS A LIGHT REFRESHMENT BY THE 1800S. "RECEIPTS" FOR MACAROONS CAN BE FOUND IN COOKERY BOOKS SINCE THE SEVENTEENTH CENTURY.

THE COLONIAL WILLIAMSBURG TAVERN COOKBOOK

176

Pecan Bars

MAKES 54 BARS

Use only the freshest nuts to make these bars. Pecans go rancid relatively quickly after shelling due to their high oil content.

FOR THE TOPPING
1 cup (2 sticks) unsalted butter
1 cup packed light brown sugar
1 cup honey
¼ cup heavy cream
3 cups coarsely chopped pecans

FOR THE BARS
¾ cup (1½ sticks) unsalted butter,
  softened
¾ cup sugar
2 large eggs
1 tablespoon finely grated lemon peel
3 cups flour
½ teaspoon baking powder

To make the topping, in a deep heavy saucepan, combine the butter, brown sugar, and honey. Bring to a boil over high heat, stirring constantly. Boil for 5 minutes and remove from the heat. Cool slightly and add the cream and pecans. Mix well and keep slightly warm until ready to bake the bars.

Preheat the oven to 350°F. and butter two 9 × 9 × 2-inch baking pans.

To make the bars, in a large bowl, beat the butter with the sugar until light and fluffy. Add the eggs and lemon peel. Mix well.

Sift the flour with the baking powder. Add to the butter mixture and beat well. Chill the dough for at least 30 minutes. Divide the dough in half. Press each half onto the bottom of the prepared pans, spreading evenly. Prick all over with a fork. Bake until the dough looks half done, about 15 minutes.

Spread the topping evenly over the partially cooked bars and bake for about 30 minutes more. Cool and cut into 1 × 2-inch bars.

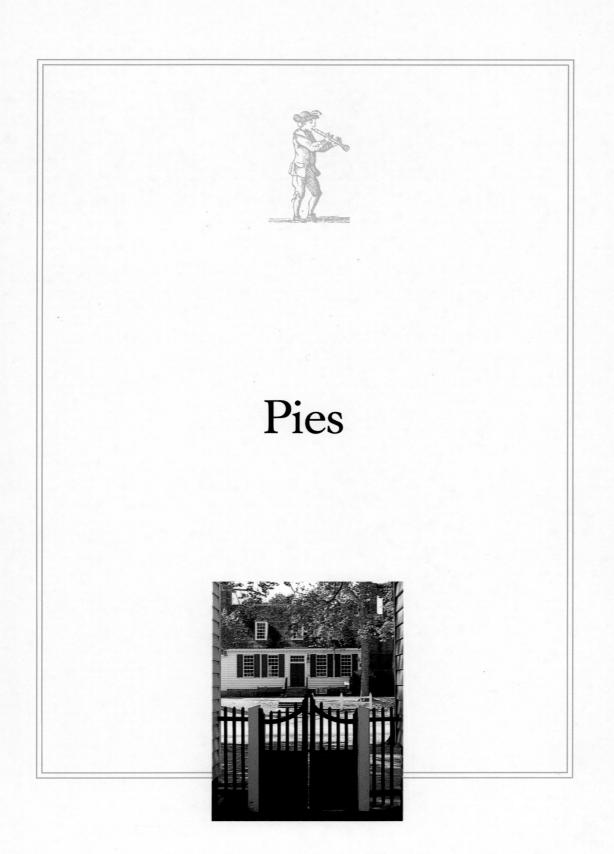

Pies

T HE English immigrants who settled eastern Virginia brought their tradition of pie eating—both savory pies of meat, fowl, fish, eggs, and vegetables encased in sturdy crusts and tender pastries filled with sweetened fruits and custards for dessert—to the New World.

Colonial housewives made pies more frequently than they baked cakes for practical reasons. Cakes required large numbers of eggs that were less plentiful in the winter than in the summer, while the ingredients for pies—fresh or preserved fruit, sugar, wheat flour, and lard—were readily available year-round.

In fashionable homes, sweet pies were part of the separate dessert course at dinner, while an apple or mince pie generally appeared along with a single course of meat, vegetables, and bread in the modest houses of small farmers and artisans. Leftover pie graced the breakfast table the next day. Then as now, apple pie (made with dried apples after the fresh ones were used up) was the favorite.

PREVIOUS PAGES, CLOCKWISE FROM TOP RIGHT: Buttermilk Pie, Chowning's Tavern Peanut Pie, King's Arms Tavern Pecan Pie, Shields Tavern Sweet Potato Pie, and Martha Washington's Cherry Pie

THE COLONIAL WILLIAMSBURG TAVERN COOKBOOK

180

Apple Pie

"In the afternoon we rode to my neighbor Harrison's where we stayed till the evening . . .
here I ate some apple pie," wrote William Byrd on June 7, 1709. Even then, the best way to
extend hospitality was to offer a visitor a slice of apple pie. Serve this most traditional of
fruit pies warm, with cinnamon- or nutmeg-flavored whipped cream.

2 recipes Pie Pastry (page 63)
1½ cups sugar
⅛ teaspoon salt
¾ teaspoon cinnamon
½ teaspoon grated nutmeg
2 tablespoons flour

6–8 tart apples, preferably Stayman or
    Rome Beauty, peeled, cored, and sliced
2 teaspoons lemon juice
½ teaspoon finely grated lemon peel
2 tablespoons (¼ stick) unsalted butter

Preheat the oven to 425°F. Roll out half the pastry to a thickness of ⅛ inch. Line a 9-inch pie pan with the pastry. Prick all over with a fork, cover with plastic wrap, and refrigerate for at least 30 minutes. For the top crust, roll out the other half of the pastry into a ⅛-inch-thick circle slightly larger than the pie pan. Place flat on a baking sheet, cover with plastic wrap, and refrigerate until the pie is assembled. (The pie pan can be lined and the top crust rolled out flat up to 2 days ahead if kept tightly covered in the refrigerator.)

In a large bowl, combine the sugar, salt, cinnamon, nutmeg, and flour. Add the apple slices and mix well to coat. Place the apple slices in the chilled pastry-lined pan, laying slices first along the outside and then working toward the center until the bottom of the pastry is covered. Continue placing the slices in the same way until the pan is filled. Sprinkle with the lemon juice and peel. Dot with the butter.

Moisten the edge of the bottom crust. Place the rolled-out pastry on top and press the edges firmly together. Crimp decoratively to seal and slash vents in the center of the crust. Bake for 15 minutes, then reduce the heat to 350°F. Bake for 40–45 minutes longer or until the apple filling is bubbling and the crust is golden brown.

Christiana Campbell's Tavern Lemon Chess Pie

"Chess" is derived from "cheese," referring to the texture of fillings in these old-fashioned pies. Traditionally, lemon chess pie was served in the winter when fresh fruit was not available. Eggs, sugar, flour, butter, and lemon flavoring were all the ingredients required to make this delicious pie. Some things never change!

1 recipe Pie Pastry (page 63)
6 large eggs
1½ cups sugar
1 tablespoon flour
1 tablespoon cornmeal

2 tablespoons (¼ stick) unsalted butter, softened
2 teaspoons grated lemon peel
¼ cup lemon juice

Preheat the oven to 350°F. Roll out the pastry to a thickness of ⅛ inch. Line a 9-inch pie pan with the pastry. Prick all over with a fork, cover with plastic wrap, and refrigerate for at least 30 minutes.

In a large bowl, beat the eggs with the sugar until light and fluffy. Beat in the flour, cornmeal, butter, lemon peel, and lemon juice. Pour the filling into the pie shell and bake until set in the center, about 45 minutes. Cool before slicing.

Lemon Tartlets

MAKES 12 TARTLETS

2 recipes Pie Pastry (page 63)
1¾ cups sugar
6–8 tablespoons lemon juice

2 tablespoons grated lemon peel
½ cup (1 stick) unsalted butter
6 large eggs, well beaten

Roll out the pastry to a thickness of ⅛ inch. Line twelve 4½ × 1½-inch tartlet molds with the pastry. Prick each all over with a fork, cover with plastic wrap, and refrigerate for at least 30 minutes.

Preheat the oven to 425°F. Fill the lined tartlet molds with parchment paper or foil. Add pie weights, dried beans, or rice to keep the pastry from puffing while cooking. Cook until lightly browned around the edges, about 10 minutes. Carefully lift off the paper or foil and the weights. Reduce the oven temperature to 375°F. and return the molds to the oven. Bake until the center of the pastry is dry and lightly browned, 8–12 minutes longer. Cool.

To prepare the filling, in a small bowl, mix the sugar, lemon juice, and lemon peel. In the top of a double boiler over hot, not boiling, water, melt the butter. Add the sugar mixture and the well-beaten eggs. Cook, stirring constantly, until very thick, about 7 minutes. Strain the mixture to remove lumps if necessary. Transfer to a bowl, cool to room temperature, then cover and chill for several hours or overnight. Spread the filling over the bottoms of the tartlet shells and serve.

Buttermilk Pie

1 recipe Pie Pastry (page 63)
6 tablespoons (¾ stick) unsalted butter, softened
1 cup sugar
3 large eggs, separated

¼ cup flour
1½ cups buttermilk
1 tablespoon lemon juice
1 teaspoon grated lemon peel

Roll out the pastry to a thickness of ⅛ inch. Line a 9-inch pie pan with the pastry. Prick all over with a fork, cover with plastic wrap, and refrigerate for at least 30 minutes.

Preheat the oven to 425°F. Fill the lined pie pan with parchment paper or foil. Add pie weights, dried beans, or rice to keep the pastry from puffing while cooking. Cook the pastry until lightly browned around the edges, about 10 minutes. Carefully lift off the paper or foil and the weights. Reduce the oven temperature to 375°F. and return the pan to the oven. Bake until the center of the pastry is white and dry, about 5 minutes longer. Cool.

Preheat the oven to 350°F.

In a large bowl, beat the butter with the sugar until light and fluffy. Add the egg yolks one at a time, beating well after each addition. Beat in the flour and mix well. Stir in the buttermilk, lemon juice, and lemon peel.

Beat the egg whites until stiff peaks form and fold into the buttermilk mixture. Pour into the pie shell and bake until the center of the pie is firm, about 50 minutes. Cool before serving.

A PROPER PIE TO THOSE IN OLD ENGLAND WAS DEEP AND HAD A TOP AND A BOTTOM CRUST. THE FRENCH, ON THE OTHER HAND, OPTED FOR A THINNER TART WITH ONLY A BOTTOM CRUST. AMERICAN PASTRY REPRESENTS THE BEST OF BOTH TRADITIONS. PIES WITH TOP AND BOTTOM CRUSTS, LATTICE TOP CRUSTS, OR NO CRUSTS AT ALL CONTAIN FILLINGS OF FRUITS, CREAMS, NUTS, BERRIES—AND MUCH, MUCH MORE.

Christiana Campbell's Tavern Rum Cream Pie

ONE 9-INCH PIE

FOR THE CRUMB CRUST
2¼ cups graham cracker crumbs
½ cup (1 stick) unsalted butter, melted
2 tablespoons sugar
½ teaspoon cinnamon

FOR THE PIE FILLING
1 envelope (1 tablespoon) unflavored
  gelatin
5 large egg yolks
1 cup sugar
⅓ cup dark rum
1½ cups heavy cream
Grated unsweetened chocolate, for
  garnish

To make the crust, in a small bowl, combine the crumbs, melted butter, sugar, and cinnamon. Press into a 9-inch pie pan and chill.

To make the filling, in a small saucepan, sprinkle the gelatin over ½ cup cold water. Let stand at room temperature for 5 minutes to soften. Heat over very low heat, stirring constantly, until dissolved.

In a large bowl, beat the egg yolks and sugar until light.

Stir the gelatin into the yolks and add the rum.

Whip the cream until it stands in soft peaks. Fold into the egg yolk and gelatin mixture. Cool until the mixture begins to set. Spoon into the crust and chill until firm enough to cut. Sprinkle with the grated chocolate before serving.

Shields Tavern Sweet Potato Pie

ONE 9-INCH PIE

Serve this delicious southern favorite with whipped cream and sprinkle with mace.

1 recipe Pie Pastry (page 63)
1½ cups canned sweet potatoes, mashed
⅔ cup sugar
2 tablespoons (¼ stick) unsalted butter, melted
½ teaspoon mace

½ teaspoon vanilla
½ teaspoon salt
2 tablespoons lemon juice
2 large eggs, lightly beaten
1 cup light cream

Roll out the pastry to a thickness of ⅛ inch. Line a 9-inch pie pan with the pastry. Prick all over with a fork, cover with plastic wrap, and refrigerate for at least 30 minutes.

Preheat the oven to 425°F. Fill the lined pie pan with parchment paper or foil. Add pie weights, dried beans, or rice to keep the pastry from puffing while cooking. Cook the pastry until lightly browned around the edges, about 10 minutes. Carefully lift off the paper or foil and the weights. Reduce the oven temperature to 375°F. and return the pan to the oven. Bake until the center of the pastry is white and dry, about 5 minutes longer. Cool.

Preheat the oven to 375°F.

In a large bowl, mix together the sweet potatoes and sugar. Beat in the butter, mace, vanilla, salt, and lemon juice. Gradually stir in the eggs and cream and mix until smooth. Pour the mixture into the pie shell and bake until a toothpick inserted in the center comes out clean, 35–40 minutes. Cool before serving.

> MACE IS THE DRIED MEMBRANE THAT SURROUNDS A NUTMEG SEED. ALONG WITH CLOVE, CINNAMON, AND NUTMEG, WILLIAMSBURG COOKS OFTEN USED MACE TO FLAVOR SWEET DISHES.

Shields Tavern Sweet Potato Pie

Chowning's Tavern Peanut Pie

ONE 9-INCH PIE

1 recipe Pie Pastry (page 63)
3 large eggs
¾ cup packed light brown sugar
1 cup light corn syrup
1 teaspoon vanilla, divided

1½ tablespoons unsalted butter, melted
¾ cup finely ground peanuts
½ cup heavy cream
1 tablespoon confectioners' sugar

Roll out the pastry to a thickness of ⅛ inch. Line a 9-inch pie pan with the pastry. Prick all over with a fork, cover with plastic wrap, and refrigerate for at least 30 minutes.

Preheat the oven to 350°F. In a large bowl, beat the eggs with the brown sugar, corn syrup, and ¾ teaspoon of the vanilla. Add the melted butter and peanuts. Pour the mixture into the pie shell and bake until the filling is set in the center and the pastry is lightly browned on the edges, 40–45 minutes. Cool on a wire rack.

Whip the cream until stiff. Add the confectioners' sugar and the remaining ¼ teaspoon vanilla. Serve warm with the whipped cream.

Black-Bottom Chocolate Pecan Pie

FOR THE PIE CRUST
1½ cups chocolate cookie crumbs
2 tablespoons sugar
6 tablespoons (¾ stick) unsalted butter,
    melted and cooled

FOR THE FILLING
4 large eggs
⅓ cup sugar
½ teaspoon salt
½ cup light corn syrup
1 tablespoon unsalted butter, melted
1 teaspoon vanilla
1 cup pecan halves
12 ounces bittersweet chocolate, melted
½ cup toasted coconut

Preheat the oven to 350°F. To make the crust, in a small bowl, mix the cookie crumbs, sugar, and melted butter. Press this mixture evenly over the bottom and sides of a 9-inch pie pan and bake for 10 minutes. Cool.

For the filling, in a large bowl, mix the eggs, sugar, salt, corn syrup, melted butter, and vanilla. Add the pecans, melted chocolate, and coconut. Pour into the pie shell and bake until firm in the center, 40–45 minutes. Cool before serving.

King's Arms Tavern Pecan Pie

*Pecans are native to Texas but have thrived for years in most of the South. They are
said to have been first planted in Virginia by Thomas Jefferson, and it is known
that George Washington included pecan trees at Mount Vernon.
When combined with eggs and sweet syrup, the dense flesh and toasty flavor of
pecans make a wonderful pie filling.*

1 recipe Pie Pastry (page 63)
4 large eggs
1 cup sugar
½ teaspoon salt
½ cup light corn syrup

4 tablespoons (½ stick) unsalted butter,
    melted
1 teaspoon vanilla
1 cup pecan halves

Roll out the pastry to a thickness of ⅛ inch. Line a 9-inch pie pan with the pastry. Prick all over with a fork, cover with plastic wrap, and refrigerate for at least 30 minutes.

Preheat the oven to 400°F.

In a large bowl, beat the eggs lightly with the sugar. Beat in the salt, corn syrup, melted butter, and vanilla. Spread the pecan halves over the bottom of the pastry and pour the filling over. Place in the oven, reduce the heat to 350°F., and bake until the filling is firm in the center, 40–50 minutes. Cool before serving.

Martha Washington's Cherry Pie

ONE 9-INCH PIE

2 recipes Pie Pastry (page 63)
1 quart sour cherries, pitted

1½ cups sugar
3 tablespoons flour

Roll out half the pastry to a thickness of ⅛ inch. Line a 9-inch pie pan with the pastry. Prick all over with a fork, cover with plastic wrap, and refrigerate for 30 minutes.

Roll out the other half of the pastry ⅛-inch thick. Cut into 1-inch-wide strips. Carefully transfer the strips to a large cookie sheet and refrigerate for 30 minutes.

In a large saucepan, combine the cherries, sugar, and flour. Cook over medium-high heat, stirring often, until the cherries begin to give off their liquid, about 10 minutes. Remove from the heat and cool slightly.

Preheat the oven to 450°F. Pour the cherry filling into the lined pie pan. Use the strips of pastry to form a decorative lattice crust over the filling. Place the pie on a baking sheet to catch spillovers and bake until the pastry is lightly browned, about 20 minutes. Reduce the heat to 375°F. and bake until the crust is well browned and the filling is bubbling, about 15 minutes. Serve warm or at room temperature.

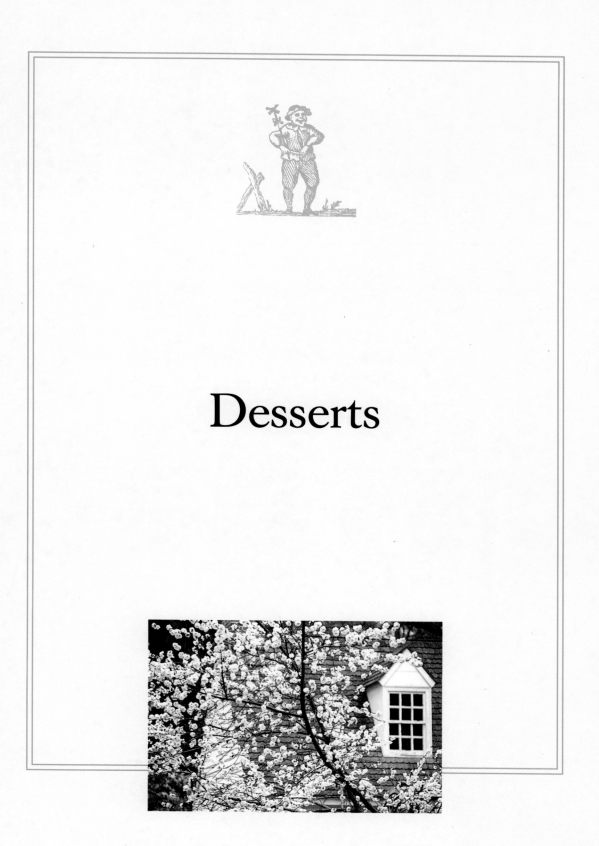

Desserts

I N taverns that catered to the wealthy, the second course at dinner was composed of sweets symmetrically arranged on expensive imported porcelain dishes that matched the guests' dessert plates. Depending on the season and the occasion, the offerings included fresh fruits, jellies, puddings, syllabubs, sweetmeats, and preserves in addition to cakes, cookies, and pies.

Well-to-do Williamsburg housewives who wanted to set an attractive dessert table must have been pleased when widow Mary Stagg opened a confectionery business. Mrs. Stagg advertised in the *Virginia Gazette* in September 1738 that she had for sale "Hartshorn Jellies and Calves-feet Jellies, fresh every Tuesday and Friday: Also Curran Jellies, & many other sorts of Fruit Jellies: Mackaroons, and Savoy Biscakes; and all sorts of Confectionery, in small Quantities, or large if wanted, every day, at very reasonable Rates."

Christmas pudding (sometimes called plum pudding), a holiday treat since medieval times, is the quintessential English pudding. Made with a mixture of minced meat or fowl, chopped suet, wine, sugar, spices, currants, raisins, almonds, and bread crumbs held together with eggs, a Christmas pudding is molded, steamed, and allowed to ripen for months before being brought out ablaze with brandy on Christmas Day.

Times and tastes change, and making grand desserts has largely been relegated to professionals. Instead of sampling a variety of sweets, most Americans, mindful of cholesterol and calories, are content with an occasional serving. The dessert recipes that follow are favored by guests at Colonial Williamsburg taverns.

PREVIOUS PAGES: Shields Tavern Syllabubs.

Ambrosia

SERVES 6

Add whole blueberries or strawberries for color and flavor.
A little dry sherry can be mixed in with the orange juice.

3 large oranges, peeled and sectioned
3 medium grapefruits, peeled and
  sectioned
½ small pineapple, peeled, cored, and
  cut into small dice

⅓ cup orange juice
¼ cup light corn syrup
½ cup flaked or shredded fresh coconut

In a large bowl, combine the oranges, grapefruits, and pineapple. In a small bowl, mix the orange juice and corn syrup and pour over the fruit. Stir gently to combine, cover with plastic wrap, and chill in the refrigerator for 2–3 hours.

Divide the fruit among 6 chilled serving dishes and spoon over the accumulated juices from the bottom of the bowl. Sprinkle each dish with a pinch of the coconut.

Chowning's Tavern Bread Pudding

SERVES 4

Day-old French or Italian bread makes delicious bread pudding.
Add some chopped candied fruit, if desired.

4 slices white bread, crusts removed
2 tablespoons (¼ stick) unsalted butter,
  softened
⅓ cup raisins
3 large eggs

½ cup sugar
1 tablespoon grated lemon peel
¼ teaspoon cinnamon
3 cups milk

Preheat the oven to 325°F. and butter a 1½-quart baking dish.

Cut the bread into thick fingers and butter one side. On the bottom of the dish, lay half the bread. Sprinkle the raisins over. Lay the remaining bread on top. In a large bowl, beat the eggs, sugar, lemon peel, and cinnamon. Stir in the milk. Pour over the bread slices and set aside to soak for 15 minutes. Bake until browned on top and set in the center, 40–45 minutes. Cool before serving.

King's Arms Tavern Meringues
with Vanilla Ice Cream and Strawberry Sauce

4 large egg whites, at room
  temperature
Pinch salt
1 cup sugar
1 teaspoon vanilla

1 pint fresh strawberries, cleaned and
  hulled
¼ cup confectioners' sugar, or more to
  taste
1 pint vanilla ice cream

Preheat the oven to 250°F. Butter and flour a large baking sheet.

In a large bowl, with an electric mixer or balloon whisk, beat the egg whites with the salt until frothy. Gradually add the sugar, beating constantly until stiff peaks form.

Transfer the meringue to a large pastry bag fitted with a star tip. Pipe 3-inch-long, 2-inch-high ovals onto the baking sheet. Bake until firm and light tan colored, about 30 minutes. Turn the oven off for 1 hour, leaving the meringues in the oven. Turn the oven on again to 250°F. and bake 30 minutes longer. Turn the oven off and leave for at least 2 hours without opening the door.

Slice the strawberries and place in a medium bowl. Sprinkle the confectioners' sugar over. Crush about a third of the berries with a fork and let the mixture stand at room temperature for 1 hour. Chill in the refrigerator until ready to serve.

To serve, arrange the meringues in individual bowls and top with a generous scoop of ice cream. Spoon or ladle the strawberries over and serve at once.

King's Arms Tavern Raisin Rice Pudding

SERVES 8

4 large eggs
¾ cup sugar
2 cups milk
1½ cups cooked rice
1½ teaspoons lemon juice

1½ teaspoons vanilla
1 tablespoon unsalted butter, melted
1 teaspoon grated nutmeg
⅔ cup seedless raisins

Preheat the oven to 350°F. and butter a 2-quart casserole.

In a large bowl, beat the eggs with the sugar and milk. Fold in the rice, lemon juice, vanilla, melted butter, nutmeg, and raisins.

Pour into the casserole and put the dish in a larger pan of boiling water. Bake until the custard is set in the center, about 45 minutes.

Plum Pudding

"Plum" in early English recipes for Christmas plum puddings referred to any dried fruit,
including raisins. So when Little Jack Horner "stuck in his thumb and
pulled out a plum," it was actually a raisin!

3 cups coarse bread crumbs
1 cup packed light brown sugar
1½ teaspoons cinnamon
1½ teaspoons grated nutmeg
¾ teaspoon allspice
½ teaspoon ground cloves
½ pound finely chopped suet
½ pound dried currants

½ pound seeded Muscat raisins
½ pound seedless raisins
¼ pound finely cut citron
¼ pound finely cut candied orange peel
6 large eggs, lightly beaten
½ cup dry white wine
1 cup brandy
Brandied Hard Sauce (recipe follows)

Butter a 2-quart pudding mold.

In a large bowl, stir together the bread crumbs, brown sugar, cinnamon, nutmeg, allspice, and cloves. Add the suet, currants, Muscat raisins, seedless raisins, citron, and candied orange peel. Mix well. Stir in the eggs and wine.

Spoon the mixture into the pudding mold and cover tightly. Place the mold on a trivet in a large kettle. Fill the kettle with enough water to come two thirds of the way up the sides of the mold. Cover the kettle and steam for 6 hours.

Remove the mold from the kettle and uncover. Cool for 20 minutes, then unmold onto a wire rack to cool completely.

Wash out the mold and line it with plastic wrap. Wrap the pudding in damp cheesecloth and return it to the mold. Prick in several places with a skewer and sprinkle with 3–4 tablespoons of the brandy. Repeat this process once a week for 3 weeks. Keep the pudding covered so that it will not dry out.

Before serving, remove the plastic wrap from the pudding. Return the pudding to the mold, cover, and place on a trivet in a large kettle. Fill the kettle with enough water to come two thirds of the way up the sides of the mold. Cover the kettle and steam for 3 hours.

Unmold the pudding. Warm 2 tablespoons of brandy and ignite it. Pour the brandy over the pudding and carry it flaming to the table. Serve with brandied hard sauce.

Brandied Hard Sauce

MAKES 2 CUPS

½ cup (1 stick) unsalted butter, softened
1½ cups confectioners' sugar
½ teaspoon vanilla

¼ teaspoon almond extract
1 tablespoon brandy
⅛ teaspoon grated nutmeg

In a large bowl, beat the butter with the sugar until light and fluffy. Beat in the vanilla and almond extracts, brandy, and nutmeg. Blend well and chill thoroughly before serving.

Peach Cobbler

SERVES 12

Use ripe but firm peaches at their peak for best results. Serve with vanilla ice cream.

FOR THE FILLING
6 cups fresh peaches (3–4 pounds),
  pitted and sliced
½ cup sugar
¼ cup cornstarch
1 teaspoon lemon juice
Pinch nutmeg
¼ teaspoon cinnamon

FOR THE TOPPING
1½ cups flour
1½ teaspoons baking powder
½ teaspoon salt
2 tablespoons sugar
¼ cup (½ stick) unsalted butter
1 large egg
⅔ cup milk

Preheat the oven to 425°F. and lightly butter a 2-quart baking dish.

In a large bowl, combine the peaches, sugar, cornstarch, lemon juice, nutmeg, and cinnamon. Stir gently until the cornstarch has dissolved. Pour the mixture into the baking dish.

Into another large bowl, sift the flour, baking powder, salt, and sugar. Cut in the butter with 2 knives or a pastry blender until the mixture resembles the texture of coarse meal.

In a small bowl, beat the egg with the milk until well blended. Stir into the flour mixture, adding just enough to thoroughly moisten the batter. Spoon the batter over the peaches and smooth the top with a large knife or spatula. Bake until the top is golden brown, 30–40 minutes. Serve warm or at room temperature.

Christiana Campbell's Tavern Tipsy Squire

SERVES 12

FOR THE CAKE
½ cup vegetable shortening
1 cup sugar
2 large eggs
2¼ cups flour
3 teaspoons baking powder
½ teaspoon salt
¾ cup milk
1 teaspoon vanilla

FOR THE CUSTARD
4 cups milk
¾ cup sugar
3 tablespoons cornstarch
⅛ teaspoon salt
3 large egg yolks
1 large egg
1 tablespoon rum
½ cup sherry

FOR SERVING
Sweetened whipped cream
Toasted slivered almonds
12 strawberries

To make the cake, preheat the oven to 350°F. and butter a 9 × 9 × 2-inch or 7 × 11 × 2-inch baking pan. Dust the inside of the pan with flour and shake out the excess.

In a large bowl, beat the shortening with the sugar until light and fluffy. Add the eggs and beat until the mixture is lemon colored.

Sift the flour with the baking powder and salt. Add the sifted dry ingredients to the sugar mixture alternately with the milk, beating well after each addition. Add the vanilla with the last addition of milk.

Pour the batter into the prepared pan. Bake the cake until a toothpick inserted in the center comes out clean, 35–40 minutes. Cool in the pan on a wire rack before serving.

To make the custard, in a medium heavy saucepan, combine the milk, sugar, cornstarch, and salt. Stir over medium heat until slightly thickened.

In a large bowl, beat the egg yolks and whole egg. Add 1 cup of the hot milk mixture to the beaten eggs. Stir well and return to the saucepan. Cook, stirring constantly without boiling, until thick and creamy, 3–5 minutes. Remove from the heat and stir in the rum and sherry. Cool completely, then chill before serving.

To serve, place a portion of the cake in a dessert bowl. Pour some of the custard over and garnish with whipped cream, almonds, and a strawberry. Serve the remaining custard on the side.

Virginia Apple Fritters

MAKES 24

2 large eggs
½ cup sugar
½ teaspoon salt
2 small apples, preferably Stayman, peeled, cored, and diced
1 cup flour
1 teaspoon baking powder

¼ teaspoon baking soda
1 teaspoon cinnamon
½ teaspoon ground ginger
1 tablespoon unsalted butter, melted
1 teaspoon vanilla
Vegetable oil for frying
Confectioners' sugar for dusting

In a large bowl, beat the eggs, sugar, and salt until light and fluffy. Stir in the apples.

Sift the flour, baking powder, and baking soda together. Add to the egg mixture. Stir in the cinnamon, ginger, melted butter, and vanilla. Cover and refrigerate for at least 2 hours.

Fill an electric deep-fat fryer half full with vegetable oil and heat to 375°F. Working in batches, drop the batter by teaspoonfuls into the hot oil. Do not fry more than 4 or 5 fritters at a time. Drain on paper towels and sprinkle with confectioners' sugar.

Shields Tavern Syllabubs

SERVES 8

Popular in early Virginia where they were considered to be beverages, these fortified dessert drinks began to lose favor in the nineteenth century as ice cream became fashionable. Having regained their popularity, syllabubs are now commonly served for dessert garnished with berries and fresh mint.

⅔ cup dry white wine
⅓ cup dry sherry
2 tablespoons grated lemon peel
¼ cup lemon juice
⅔ cup sugar

2 cups heavy cream
Several sprigs fresh mint, for garnish
An assortment of fresh berries, for
  garnish

In a large bowl, combine the wine, sherry, lemon peel, and lemon juice. Add the sugar and stir until dissolved.

Whip the cream in a large bowl until it forms medium-stiff peaks. Fold into the wine mixture. Spoon into 8 wineglasses, cover with plastic wrap, and refrigerate overnight. The mixture will separate and be ready to enjoy the next day. Garnish with fresh mint and berries.

To make whipt Syllabubs

TAKE A QUART OF CREAM, . . . A PINT OF SACK, AND THE JUICE OF TWO LEMONS; SWEETEN IT TO YOUR PALATE, PUT IT INTO A BROAD EARTHEN PAN, AND WITH A WHISK WHIP IT; AS THE FROTH RISES, TAKE IT OFF WITH A SPOON, AND LAY IT IN YOUR SYL-LABUB GLASSES; BUT FIRST YOU MUST SWEETEN SOME CLARET, SACK, OR WHITE WINE, AND STRAIN IT, AND PUT SEVEN OR EIGHT SPOONFULS OF THE WINE INTO YOUR GLASSES, AND THEN GENTLY LAY IN YOUR FROTH.

E. Smith, The Compleat Housewife, *1742*

Trifle

Although this recipe has been modified over the years, it has remained remarkably similar
to its 1798 inspiration from Rules Restaurant in London.

FOR THE CUSTARD SAUCE
2 cups milk
½ teaspoon vanilla
5 large egg yolks
¼ cup sugar

FOR THE TRIFLE
2 dozen ladyfingers or 1 layer of sponge
   cake, cut into fingers
2 teaspoons finely grated lemon peel
¼ cup brandy
1 cup dry sherry
1 cup pitted sour cherries
2 cups heavy cream, whipped until stiff
   peaks form

To make the custard sauce, into a small saucepan, pour the milk. Heat over medium-high heat until bubbles form around the edges of the pan. Remove from the heat and stir in the vanilla.

In a medium bowl, whisk the egg yolks with the sugar until thickened and lemon colored. Slowly stir in the hot milk.

Return the custard to the saucepan. Stir constantly over medium-low heat until the custard is thick enough to leave a trail when a finger is drawn across the back of a wooden spoon, 5–7 minutes. Cool completely, then chill for several hours before assembling the trifle.

Line a large glass bowl with half the ladyfingers. Sprinkle the lemon peel over. Evenly pour half the brandy and sherry over. Cover with half the sour cherries and let stand at room temperature for 1 hour. Ladle or spoon half the custard sauce over and repeat the layers. Chill for at least 12 hours before serving, topped with the whipped cream.

> SPONGE CAKE SOAKED WITH BRANDY AND SHERRY, LAYERS OF VANILLA CUSTARD AND FRUIT OR JAM, AND WHIPPED CREAM FOR THE TOPPING ARE THE TIME-HONORED COMPONENTS OF A PROPER TRIFLE.

Ice Creams

THE first mention of ice cream in early America appears in the diary of Virginian William Black. His account of dinner at the home of Maryland Governor Thomas Bladen in Annapolis on May 19, 1744, leaves no doubt that Black was impressed: "We were Received by his Excellency and his Lady in the Hall, . . . then the Scene was chang'd to a Dining Room, where you saw a Table in the most Splendent manner set out with a Great Variety of Dishes, all serv'd up in the most Elegant way, after which came a Dessert no less Curious; Among the Rarities of which it was Compos'd, was some fine Ice Cream which, with the Strawberries and Milk, eat most Deliciously."

In 1758, when Francis Fauquier was serving as Lieutenant Governor of Virginia, a hailstorm "broke every pane of glass on the north side his house, and destroyed all his garden things intirely." The next day, Governor Fauquier "cooled his wine, and froze cream" with some of the hailstones.

The storm may have been the incentive for building an icehouse at the Governor's Palace. Although the date of construction isn't known, the icehouse was repaired shortly after the next governor, Lord Botetourt, arrived in the fall of 1768. The inventory of Governor Botetourt's personal belongings includes "16 pewter ice Moulds" among the items in the kitchen, suggesting that dinners at the Palace easily rivaled the one William Black attended and likely included ice cream.

Chowning's Tavern Black Walnut Ice Cream

MAKES 1 ½ QUARTS

Farmers on the East Coast, where the black walnut is native, spent many a winter evening before an open fire cracking and eating walnuts. A nut of such fine taste just had to find its way into ice cream.

8 large egg yolks
1¼ cups sugar
Dash salt
2 cups milk

2 cups heavy cream
1 teaspoon black walnut flavoring
1 cup chopped black walnuts

In a large bowl, beat the egg yolks with the sugar until thick and lemon colored. Add the salt. In a large saucepan, combine the milk and cream and heat over medium-high heat. When bubbles form around the edges, just before the boiling point, remove the saucepan from the heat. Gradually pour the hot milk and cream over the egg mixture, beating constantly. Pour back into the saucepan and cook over medium heat, stirring constantly, until thickened, about 5 minutes. Stir in the black walnut flavoring and the walnuts. Remove from the heat and set aside to cool.

Freeze in an electric ice cream maker following the manufacturer's instructions. Pack as freezing instructions direct and allow to ripen for at least 3 hours before serving.

Shields Tavern Coconut Ice Cream

MAKES 1 ½ QUARTS

½ cup sugar
2 (15-ounce) cans cream of coconut

1 tablespoon rum

In a small saucepan, mix the sugar and ½ cup water to make a simple syrup. Warm over medium-high heat, stirring gently, until the sugar has dissolved. Remove from the heat and cool.

In a large bowl, mix the syrup, cream of coconut, and rum. Chill in the refrigerator until very cold. Freeze in an electric ice cream maker following the manufacturer's instructions.

King's Arms Tavern Greengage Plum Ice Cream

MAKES 3 QUARTS

Considered one of the world's best varieties, the greengage plum reached France during the reign of François I (1494–1547) and is still known there as "Reine Claude," after his wife. The English name comes from Sir Thomas Gage, who received stocks from France early in the eighteenth century. It seems only natural that the plum found its way to America, where it is as prized as it is in Europe. Greengage plum is one of the most popular ice creams at the King's Arms today. Substitute any variety of seasonal fresh or canned plums if the greengage is not to be found.

5 large eggs, separated
1½ cups sugar, divided
2 cups milk
3 cups fresh or canned (1 pound, 12 ounces) greengage plums, drained and pitted

1½ pints light cream or half-and-half
⅓ cup lemon juice

In a large bowl, beat the egg yolks with 1 cup of the sugar. Warm the milk over medium-high heat until bubbles form around the edges. Pour 1 cup of the hot milk over the beaten egg yolks, stirring until well blended. Return the mixture to the hot milk. Cook over medium heat until thick enough to coat the back of a metal spoon, 5 minutes. Do not boil or the mixture will separate. Cool completely.

In another large bowl, beat the egg whites with the remaining ½ cup sugar until they form stiff peaks. Fold into the egg and milk mixture.

In a food processor or blender, puree the plums. Add the pureed plums, cream, and lemon juice gradually to the egg mixture.

Freeze in an electric ice cream maker following the manufacturer's instructions.

NOTE: Allow the ice cream to ripen for at least 4 hours after freezing to bring out the delicate greengage plum flavor. If fresh plums are used, they should be blanched for 60 seconds in hot water before the skins are removed.

Mrs. Randolph's Frozen Lemonade

MAKES 1 QUART

Here, Mrs. Randolph's eighteenth-century recipe has been streamlined and the egg whites left out, but Colonial Williamsburg chefs hope that she would be pleased with the results.

1 cup sugar
½ cup light corn syrup

1 (6-ounce) can frozen lemonade
    concentrate
1 tablespoon grated lemon peel

In a large saucepan, combine the sugar and 3 cups water. Bring to a boil over medium-high heat and boil for 5 minutes. Remove from the heat and stir in the corn syrup, concentrate, and lemon peel. Cool completely. Strain the mixture into the freezer container of an electric ice cream maker and freeze according to the manufacturer's instructions.

Christiana Campbell's Tavern Fig Ice Cream

MAKES 3 QUARTS

4 large eggs, separated
1¼ cups sugar
2 cups milk
3 tablespoons lemon juice

2 cups light cream or half-and-half
½ cup sherry
1 teaspoon vanilla
1 quart figs, crushed or pureed

In a large bowl, beat the egg yolks with half the sugar. In a medium saucepan over medium-high heat, heat the milk. When bubbles form around the edges, just before the boiling point, remove the saucepan from the heat. Gradually pour the hot milk over the egg mixture, beating constantly. Pour back into the saucepan and cook over medium heat, stirring constantly, until thick, about 3–5 minutes. Remove from the heat and set aside to cool.

Beat the egg whites with the remaining sugar until frothy. Pour the cooked egg and milk mixture into the egg whites, stirring constantly. Stir in the lemon juice. Add the cream, sherry, vanilla, and figs and mix well.

Freeze in an electric ice cream maker following the manufacturer's instructions.

King's Arms Tavern Peppermint Ice Cream

MAKES 1½ QUARTS

2 cups milk
1 cup sugar
1 teaspoon peppermint extract
4 large eggs

2 cups heavy cream
¾ cup crushed peppermint candy
Red food coloring (optional)

Heat the milk in a medium saucepan over medium-high heat. When bubbles form around the edges, just before the boiling point, remove the saucepan from the heat and stir in the sugar. Stir to dissolve. Add the peppermint extract and set the mixture aside to cool completely.

In a large bowl, beat the eggs with the cream until light and fluffy. Pour in the milk mixture and mix well. Fold in the peppermint candy. Add a few drops of the food coloring if desired. Cover and refrigerate until well chilled. Freeze in an electric ice cream maker following the manufacturer's instructions.

Rum Raisin Ice Cream

MAKES 1½ QUARTS

2 cups raisins
1½ cups dark rum
8 egg yolks
½ cup sugar

2 cups milk
2 cups whipping cream
1 teaspoon vanilla

In a small bowl, combine the raisins and rum and let stand for 3–4 hours.

In a large stainless steel bowl, beat the egg yolks and sugar until thick and creamy. In a medium saucepan over medium-high heat, scald the milk. Gradually whisk the milk into the egg mixture. Mix well. Into a larger pan containing simmering water, place the bowl with the egg mixture and cook, stirring constantly, until the custard thickens slightly, about 10 minutes. Remove from the heat.

Drain the raisins and reserve. Add the rum to the custard mixture and cool completely. Just before freezing, add the whipping cream and vanilla. Freeze in an ice cream maker following the manufacturer's instructions. Add the raisins just before the ice cream freezes firm.

Beverages

EARLY Virginians believed alcoholic beverages to be wholesome, refreshing, beneficial, and often safer to drink than the water. Given a choice of strong drink, they favored rum, "good Barbadoes" being preferred over "New England and other bad rum." "In great heat, in great cold, and during severe work, this heart-strengthener is indispensable," noted one observer. Virginians also drank quantities of imported wines (Madeira, claret, and Port were especially popular), beer and ale from London and Bristol, brandies from France, and arrack imported from the East Indies. Cheaper, locally produced beverages such as apple cider and small beer made from molasses, hops, wheat bran, and yeast, which was lower in alcoholic content than imported strong beers, were also popular.

Punch was popular among all Virginians. Made from a distilled liquor, lemon juice, sugar, and water, punch was served cold. The price varied depending on which spirit was used. It was common for men to drink directly from the bowl and then pass it on to the next drinker.

Virginians also drank water with rum, called grog, which was favored by the common sort and distributed to slaves during the heavy work of harvesting; toddies of water mixed with rum and sugar; and flip, a hot drink of strong beer to which rum and sugar were added. Christmas festivities weren't complete without eggnog and wassail.

Tea, coffee, and chocolate appeared at breakfast in homes and taverns. First drunk exclusively by the gentry, tea and coffee surpassed chocolate in popularity as the lower sort adopted the behavior of their betters. Politics interfered with the consumption of imported tea in the 1770s, but Virginians quickly resumed drinking it after the Revolution ended.

Chowning's Tavern Mulled Apple Cider

SERVES 8

8 cups fresh apple cider
1 cup packed light brown sugar
½ cup lemon juice

½ teaspoon grated nutmeg
1 cinnamon stick
8 whole cloves

In a large saucepan, combine the cider, sugar, lemon juice, and nutmeg. Tie the cinnamon stick and the cloves in a cheese-cloth bag and place in the pan. Simmer over medium-high heat for 10 minutes. Remove the bag of spices and serve hot.

CIDER WAS ENORMOUSLY POPULAR WITH THE "MIDDLING SORT" IN EARLY VIRGINIA. APPLES GROWN ON PLANTATIONS NEAR WILLIAMSBURG PROVIDED THE JUICE, WHICH WAS FRESH WHEN FIRST PRESSED BUT QUICKLY FERMENTED.

Rummer

SERVES 1

1¼ ounces dark rum
¾ ounce peach brandy
¾ ounce apricot brandy

Slice of orange, for garnish
Maraschino cherry, for garnish

Into an 8-ounce glass pour the rum, peach brandy, and apricot brandy. Add ice cubes as desired. Garnish with the orange slice and maraschino cherry.

Wine Punch

SERVES 12

1 (750-ml) bottle red wine
1 cup orange juice
1 cup pineapple juice

2 lemons, sliced and seeded
3 oranges, sliced and seeded

In a large bowl, combine the red wine, orange juice, pineapple juice, lemons, and oranges. Pour over a block of ice.

Eggnog

The origin of this most festive of Christmas drinks is the old English milk punch much enjoyed in the eighteenth century. This traditional recipe is best served cold in a large crystal bowl with a silver ladle.

6 large eggs, separated
½ cup sugar
2 cups heavy cream
1 cup milk

½ cup bourbon
½ cup brandy
½ cup light rum
Grated nutmeg, for garnish

In a large bowl, beat the egg yolks with the sugar until thick. Gradually add the cream, milk, bourbon, brandy, and rum. Chill. In a large bowl, beat the whites until stiff peaks form. Fold the whites into the cream mixture and refrigerate until well chilled. Sprinkle with nutmeg before serving.

King's Arms Tavern Berry Shrub

SERVES 8

3 cups cranberry juice
¾ cup apple juice

1 pint raspberry sherbet
8 sprigs fresh mint, for garnish

In a large bowl, combine the cranberry and apple juices and chill thoroughly. Serve in tall glasses and top each with a scoop of sherbet. Garnish each glass with a sprig of mint.

Christiana Campbell's Tavern Wassail

SERVES 20

Ves heill is Norse for "be in good health." The early English toast to someone's health has become a popular part of the special Christmas celebrations at Colonial Williamsburg. Whole cloves, allspice berries, or shavings of mace can be added or substituted as desired.

1 cup sugar
4 cinnamon sticks
3 lemon slices, plus additional slices for garnish
2 cups pineapple juice

2 cups orange juice
½ cup lemon juice
6 cups dry red wine
1 cup dry sherry

In a large saucepan, combine the sugar, cinnamon sticks, 3 lemon slices, and ½ cup water and bring to a boil over high heat. Boil for 5 minutes and strain. Discard the cinnamon sticks and lemon slices.

In a large saucepan, mix the pineapple, orange, and lemon juices, wine, and sherry and bring to a simmer over medium heat. Do not boil.

Combine the wine mixture with the sugar syrup, garnish with lemon slices, and serve hot.

Acknowledgments

Grateful thanks for their many contributions go to John Askew, Barbara Bilderback, Lynwood Blizzard, Ralph Bouton, Willie Coles, Barbara Conrad, Patricia Gibbs, Judy Hornby, Natalie Larson, Laura Martinsen and the staff of the Benjamin Powell House, Mike McGilvary, Beth Putnam, Joe Sciegaj, Janine Skerry, Bill Wandersee, Flo-Ann Weaver, and Tanya Wilson at Colonial Williamsburg; Maggie Hinders and Jean Lynch at Clarkson Potter; Jim Cremins, CEO, Virginia FoodService Group; and Michelle Erickson and Rob Hunter, Period Designs, whose objects appear on pages 34, 39, 46, 78, 83, 95, 107, 114, and 147. Photographs on pages 59, 79, 119, 155, and 211 are by Colonial Williamsburg photographers Dave Doody and Tom Green.

Index